the island
in the CONFLUENCE

the island in the CONFLUENCE

MARC ENGELHARDT

WESTBOW
PRESS
A DIVISION OF THOMAS NELSON

Library of Congress Control Number: 2012909250

WestBow Press books may be ordered through booksellers or by contacting:

WestBow Press
A Division of Thomas Nelson
1663 Liberty Drive
Bloomington, IN 47403
www.westbowpress.com
1-(866) 928-1240

ISBN: 978-1-4497-5365-8 (sc)
ISBN: 978-1-4497-5367-2 (hc)
ISBN: 978-1-4497-5366-5 (e)

All Bible quotes are from The Holy Bible: English Standard Version. *2001 Wheaton: Standard Bible Society*

Printed in the United States of America

WestBow Press rev. date: 05/25/2012

Contents

Preface

This book is the culmination of several years of observation, study, presentations, and discussion with friends. I have put it all together in the hope that it will benefit the Bride of Christ, of which I am so grateful to be a part. Some of the ideas in this book will not be new to many leaders in the Church—after all, I'm not making this stuff up—then again, many of the ideas may be new to the reader. My desire is to make connections among these ideas so that we may grasp the reality of the Church's situation.

The book is primarily written in the way I think—that is, inductively, with an infusion of story. The result is that the text will likely raise questions in the reader's mind that are eventually answered as the reader moves through the book. The story is mixed in to ground the theory and give examples of the concepts.

While this is not intended to be a scholarly book I have included a few footnotes for two purposes: to give credit where credit is due and to include my tangential thoughts. These thoughts do not belong in the main text but give more color to the overall picture. If desired, the reader could ignore all the footnotes and miss nothing of the main thrust of the book.

Contemporary usage tends no longer to regard the masculine pronoun as all-inclusive. I can understand some of the reasons that this has happened. My options instead were to use the cumbersome "he or she," the confusing "s/he," or to use both "he" and "she" inclusively. I chose to use "he" and "she" randomly, both as inclusive pronouns.

Since this has been an ongoing project for years, I undoubtedly will forget to thank some people who have given me insight into this topic or have encouraged me. I ask you for grace. For now, I wish to acknowledge, in no particular order, those of whom I am most aware who have helped me: my wife, Lauren, who understands that not everyone understands me; my grace-full parents, Tim and Kathy; Lauren's parents, Tom and Joan; the rest of my family members, who have been a source of love, support, and prayer; all the folks at Reconcile Church and Brookfield Lutheran Church; the people committed to Regeneration and its discussion; Melissa Ritterbusch my editor; my faithful sounding board, the Rev. Ryan Alvey; my mentor on the bike and in theology, the Rev. Dr. Jeffery Kloha; and my mentor in the parish, the Rev. Roger Heintz. Anything that I write that makes sense is the result of all of their help and influence. If something comes across as confusing and wrong, well, that's all me.

My writing this book is evidence that Jesus redeems and restores people. The potential of His Church, and the people who make it up, is far more than most give credit. This book is a beginning of a discussion; if you want to discuss it more, please visit https://mengelhardt. wordpress.com/ and http://www.facebook.com/pages/The-Island-in-the-Confluence/305794349461809.

Marc Engelhardt
February, 2012

Introduction

The city of Milwaukee was centered and founded at the junction of three rivers. The Kinnickinnic comes from the south; the Menomonee flows from the west; and the Milwaukee surges from the north. The point where they meet is a confluence, surrounded by land where German, Polish, and French settlers of the 1800s worked together to start a city. Milwaukee not only holds a confluence of rivers but also a confluence of communities.

Technically speaking, a Confluence is a coming or flowing together, meeting, or gathering at one point; the flowing together of two or more streams; the place where two streams meet. Whereas the term defines a gathering point, I also find the Confluence to be a fitting term for describing the state of individual participation in communities today. Now more than ever before, people have access to pick, choose, and customize the communities in which they take part. The communities come together in a Confluence, and individuals wade in the water. That reality is not inherently good or bad, but it does have real consequences that influence how individuals regard themselves, how they regard each other, and how they see the role of community fitting into their lives.

The Confluence's direct effect on the Church is clear. The Church is a community that has something to say about personal identity, as well as how people view and interact with the world. The idea of the Confluence then raises some major questions for the Church: What is the role of the Church in the Confluence? How should Christians act in the Confluence? How do we effectively share the Gospel in the Confluence?

In order to address these questions, we first need to understand the situation in which we find ourselves. We will first take a broad look at the development of individual identity in Western culture during the past three hundred years, and then we will assess how that individual identity interacts within the Fluid Confluence of Communities.

The next step will be to identify the marks of the Kingdom Community. We will then look at the role the Kingdom Community plays in the life of the individual in the Confluence. After having all of that in place, I believe we can then address some concerns about mission, discipleship, and church structure. In the end, the ideal is to arrive at some practical, adaptable strategies to engage Western culture more effectively with the Good News of Jesus Christ.

The Bride of Christ, the Church, will not die out or fade. It will continue to flourish, grow, and take shapes we may never have imagined. Jesus is faithful and keeps His promises. We need to follow Him wherever He leads, work with what He has given us, and look as He describes. Too often we are in front of Him, creating barriers, and telling Him what we want. How long can the Church continue with such an attitude before pieces of us fall off the Body and are no longer part of the Bride? Let's take an honest look at ourselves and be willing to follow Christ faithfully, with the courage of the Holy Spirit, into the world in which we live.

Part One:
The Rise of the Individual

When I have the chance to travel, I am not one to check out the tourist spots. I am not big on sightseeing unless it involves the awe of creation. What I like to do is experience a little bit of the life of the people I am visiting. Where and what do they like to eat? What is the local beer of choice? What do they consider a good time? What are the morning and evening routines? Experiencing these things allows me a vacation from myself, but, for the people I am visiting, the routine is the same—except for the oddity that I am tagging along. I get to observe a different culture, while they don't even realize they are participating in one.

Experiencing a different culture generally involves something weird, new, wonderful, perplexing, or annoying. When such things occur and I consciously notice them, I have a choice either to become an observer or a judge. If I become an observer, I notice the difference then seek to discover why it is a difference in the first place. How or why does such a thing strike me as abnormal?

Being an observer requires introspection. One needs to be open to tracing back the path of an initial reaction and be willing to recognize built-in biases as *different*, not necessarily *correct*. In short, when one becomes an observer of others, one becomes an observer of oneself. To be an observer takes work, and I believe in its purest form it is impossible.[1]

To take the role of a judge is one of the most natural things in the world. In the role of a judge, I become the norm. Everything is measured against my values, ideas, and concepts of how the world works. Nothing happens beyond my initial response to stimuli. I judge it against what I find to be normal, routine, awful, simple, or pleasing, and the process ends there.

In this venture I am asking you to assume the role of observer rather than judge. Doing so may be somewhat difficult because the assignment does not entail visiting another culture; instead, you will be attempting to observe your own. By attempting to observe rather than judge, you will be able to gather insights into your world that are otherwise unobtainable. If you remain a judge, you will be unable to see past yourself, and you will likely miss much of the hope this book provides.

My goal in Part One is to illustrate that many of the characteristics of thought we find to be innate are actually somewhat recent developments in history. In other words, we have not always thought this way, and what you may believe to be the very bedrock of your thought processes has in fact developed over time. We are so immersed in these thought processes from birth that we can easily take them to be simply the way the world works. That is why it will take some work to be an observer, but I believe the work is well worth the payoff. Hope exists beyond the horizon of our current context.

Some folks would prefer an in-depth look at the development of thought and culture in Western society. Others are not interested in the history and want to get right to the practical applications. We are going to take the middle path and look at history, in admittedly broad strokes, on our way to the applications. To begin then, we will take a look at a few of the major contributing factors from the past three hundred years.

Defining Terms

In the past I have had some "different" hairstyles. Most people these days find it a little hard to believe, since all they have ever known is me with short, not-quite-buzz-cut hair. I try to tell them that the only thing that trumps my creativity is my laziness, and frankly my past hairstyles were a ton of work. Bleaching one's hair and dying it a different color of the rainbow every three or four weeks is time-consuming, and, unless you have had one, you have no idea how high-maintenance a mohawk can be. Dreadlocks, or the fabled reverse mullet, are even worse. Some people would call my hairstyle choices rebellion; some would call them an expression of my personality; and still others would call them commonplace. Most everyone would agree that I was at least attempting to assert my individuality.

Individuality is highly prized in Western society. Hipsters and youth culture provide today's examples of people seeking to be recognized as unique individuals, while cultural icons, like James Dean and the American cowboy, are timeless. What all of these examples have in common, while not necessarily explicitly said, is that being an individual is a defining aspect of one's life.

For the hipster today, life is all about not following trends or trying to be cool.[2] Instead, the hipster cuts her own path and makes her own choices. The idealized figure of James Dean, in some respects, is similar to the hipster: he not only stands out from the general populace but also bucks and questions authority. The American cowboy embodies the ideas of "not being fenced in" and "being one's own man." The cowboy is also intermingled with Manifest Destiny, a concept that has evolved over time and become deeply ingrained in the American psyche.

These few examples illustrate the cult of the individual in the West.[3] It is ingrained in us. Individuality is not just about people who look different, either. No, it is lurking underneath the consciousness of the average Joe. He may not stick out visually, but his identity is wrapped up in the Americanized idea of being an individual. He is the type of person with the mentality of being a self-made man who has a right to whatever he wants as long as he is within the law.[4] In his view, other people in society are not allowed to judge him or his actions, or tell him what do. I liken this rampant individualism to him being the star of his own movie. The movie is his life, and everyone else is an extra his movie.

Most of us, if we are honest, find ourselves starring in our own movie. We may strive not to be the star all the time, but it sure seems like a role we were built to play. The question is: why? Is it just sinful nature? Have people always been this way? Well, yes and no. It is certainly sinful nature, and, to a point, people have always placed themselves in the starring roles of their lives. This makes sense if you take pride to be the root of sin. After all, Adam and Eve wanted to be like God, and in doing so they received the opposite of pride—that is, shame. In the West, though, a shift in thought in the last three hundred years has amounted to the emphasis of the individual above all things.[5] This shift has swelled individuals' desires to be the stars of their own movies more than at any other time in history. By observing this shift, we can see how the present state came about then grasp how to deal with it.

Before we dig into the Rise of the Individual, we must juxtapose individuality and community. Definitions of community are broad and multifaceted. If one asked ten different sociologists or anthropologists for a definition, one likely would have ten different answers. For our purposes in studying community, we will focus on the aspects of shared likeness, character, and interests: community takes place when two or more people share interests, beliefs, values, backgrounds, or goals and communicate about the aspects of their lives that they share.

Having established at least a surface-level identification of the cult of the individual, as well as having defined community, we can now take a look back over the past three hundred years and trace the development of individualism, a doctrine that raises the interest of the individual above all other controlling factors.[6] It is a belief that is held deeply in the post-Enlightenment world, and it affects the everyday decisions and actions of most people in the West. It influences how most people see the world working. Individualism is the driving force of the hipster, the "Rebel without a Cause," and the American cowboy, among others.

History

We will start at what many people consider the beginning with a brief synopsis of the contributions of John Locke, David Hume, Søren

Kierkegaard, Friedrich Nietzsche, and Manifest Destiny. First, though, let's take a look at Jake, today's typical, hipster-type twentysomething:

Jake's usual ensemble consists of tight corduroy pants, penny loafers, and ironic t-shirts. He is also currently sporting a well-waxed handlebar moustache and glasses that are very oversized for his head. Jake likes nothing more than to go to the corner bar with his friends to drink cheap beer and shoot pool.

Jake has lived with his girlfriend, Loraine, for four years. They love each other but do not want to put any constraints on their relationship, although they are monogamous and want to stay that way. They just don't see why getting married is important; it wouldn't change their lives. Jake's parents are divorced, and now Jake's father is living with his significant other. Jake's father came out as being homosexual when Jake was in high school. He believes that his dad can't change who he is and hopes he is happy, but they don't talk much anymore. Jake spends a lot more time with his mom.

Jake seems to have been in school forever. He has been fascinated with plants his whole life, so he currently is working towards his masters degree in botany. He is amazed at how the discovery of new facts happens all the time. He plans on doing research when he graduates but isn't sure what that will mean about his relationship with Loraine. He knows he will have to move—likely out of the country. He hopes that the relationship will work out and that Loraine will come along, but he isn't going to push her.

Jake is an adventurous guy who likes to try new things. He is currently in a kickball league and plays banjo in a bluegrass band, "The Moon Shines Heavy." He is acquainted with a lot of people and could spend hours every day on social media websites, but he doesn't really know most of the people in his life. He sits and talks face to face with only about four people on a regular basis, his mother and Loraine being two of them.

During class one day, the instructor makes a conclusion about the defense systems of a particularly interesting conifer then backhandedly insults anyone who believes in the existence of a god of creation. That sentiment is nothing new to Jake: he too thinks creation myths are just folklore, but the way this instructor states it strikes him as wrong. Is it so self-evident there is no god? Who says? Does evolution negate a spiritual existence necessarily? Loraine believes in a higher power, and weird things happen in their guestroom that she says are the work of a ghost. If ghosts were real, wouldn't that mean that a spiritual element exists? He has certainly tried, but he can't explain away all the weird things that happen in their guestroom.

Jake's life is rather typical today. Most of us can probably identify with at least part of his life, or we know someone who can. We are left with questions like: why does Jake react the way he does in class? Why not get married? If he knows so many people, why does he only *really* talk to so few? To understand why he reacts this way, we need to understand how he thinks and perceives life. Beyond the technological differences, Jake would not have perceived the world three hundred years ago the way he does now. To understand him better, we need to see how his way of thought has been formed over the last three hundred years.

A change in thought started to take place in the 1500s—the century of the Reformation, when a few theologians, the most prominent of whom was Martin Luther, confronted the Catholic Church about aspects of its doctrine and practice that were inconsistent with Scripture. One of the results of the Reformation was the decentralization of power in the Church. Another result was the beginning of the first real separation of church and government in the West since the time of Constantine about 1200 years earlier. Both of these changes influenced how people saw themselves and their place in the world.

Up until and during the 1500s, the class into which one was born determined much of one's future—whether one would be poor or wealthy, a farmer or a tradesmen, a commoner or part of the aristocracy. Birthplace determined what religion one would be, and, after the Reformation, it also could determine what "stream" of Christianity one would be. Money could buy education, but moving up in society was still limited and not likely to happen within one generation. In short, much of a person's life was predetermined by society's expectations and restraints. This was the world of John Locke, our first contributor to the Rise of the Individual.

John Locke

Many consider John Locke to be the father of the Enlightenment. His contributions to philosophical, scientific, and political thought paved the way for the Modern Era. Locke may have lived more than three hundred years ago, but his work influences people like Jake in the West today.

Born in 1632 in Wrington, England, Locke was well educated and a peer of great thinkers like Robert Boyle and Isaac Newton.[7] He saw merit in the alternative thinking of René Descartes compared to the Aristotelian philosophies of the dwindling Reformation era.[8] He also was an observer of the revolution in England in the mid-1600s that transferred the power of the government from the King to the Parliament.[9]

Locke developed his philosophy as he watched society change. Two elements of his philosophy that we want to consider are *tabula rasa* and the God-given rights of the individual. First, we will take a look at *tabula rasa*, or blank slate.

"Locke holds that the mind is a *tabula rasa* or blank sheet until experience in the form of sensation and reflection provide the basic materials—simple ideas—out of which most of our more complex knowledge is constructed."[10] In other words, knowledge is formed from experience via observation alone. To oversimplify it: one can understand things only through observation, not through the workings of some sort of innate logic. Locke clearly believes, however, that God-given tools exist to process the observable world.

The belief in the blank slate eventually leads to the empirical method of thought in which knowledge is based on verifiable observation or experience alone. Note that the emphasis is not *necessarily* on firsthand experience or observation alone; instead, the emphasis is on *verifiable* observation or experience. "For the individual, Locke wants each of us to use reason to search after truth rather than simply accept the opinion of authorities or be subject to superstition. He wants us to proportion assent to propositions to the evidence for them."[11] We will see shortly how Locke's empiricism and questioning of kingship contributed to the Enlightenment through the work of David Hume.

While Locke is concerned with how the individual observes and knows the world, he also is preoccupied with how the individual interacts with the world and, in turn, how the world interacts with the individual. Locke holds that God gives each individual the right to live equally, according to God's pleasure:

> ...by [God's] order and about his business, [people] are his property whose workmanship they are, made to last during his, not one another's pleasure: and being furnished with like faculties, sharing all in one community of nature, there cannot be supposed any subordination among us, that may authorize us to destroy one another, as if we were made for one another's uses, as the inferior ranks of creatures are for ours.[12]

Earlier, Locke describes how this equality manifests itself in society:

> The state of nature has a law of nature to govern it, which obliges everyone: and reason which is that law, teaches all mankind who will but consult it, that being all equal and independent, no one ought to harm another in his life, health, liberty or possession . . . .[13]

William Uzgalis, a Locke scholar, summarizes then:

> If God's purpose for me on earth is my survival and that of
> my species, and the means to that survival are my life, health,
> liberty, and property — then clearly I don't want anyone to
> violate my rights to these things. Equally, considering other
> people, who are my natural equals, I should conclude that
> I should not violate their rights to life, liberty, health, and
> property. This is the law of nature.[14]

For Locke, all people are equal under God and have a right to survive
in peace. Survival and peace are protected as each individual is allowed
to pursue life, health, liberty, and possessions while not infringing on
another individual's pursuit. For Americans this language should sound
very familiar. The Declaration of Independence states, "We hold these
truths to be self-evident, that all men are created equal, that they are
endowed by their Creator with certain unalienable Rights, that among
these are Life, Liberty and the pursuit of Happiness." The founding
fathers of the United States were clearly influenced by the work of John
Locke.

John Locke's influence on Jake is clear, too. His self-expression, identity,
and approval of—albeit distant relationship with—his father reflect his
view of equal rights. Jake may have wanted a solid, intact family structure
without divorce, and his relationship with his father appears damaged;
however, Jake understands that his father is pursuing his own dreams and
will not stand in his way.

Jake also questions authority. His instructor's offhanded remark causes
him to doubt his instructor's perspective and then question the scientific
community's status quo stance on God's existence. Pursuant to Locke's
initiation of individual-centric thought, the suspicion of authority begins
to gain steam with David Hume and is evident among philosophers going
forward through the history of thought.

David Hume

Now we will see why Jake is so put off by the instructor's comment. The comment is based on an assumed belief and not backed by evidence. It doesn't sit well with Jake because he can think of possible evidence in his life for the spiritual world—Jake needs proof from the instructor. No one contributes more to the "prove it to me" quality of the Individual than David Hume.

David Hume lived from 1711 to 1776 and is best known as a British philosopher and great empiricist. Hume built on the work of people like John Locke, but he took empiricism a step further. Hume's first principle, also known as the "Copy Principle,"[15] is based on the notion that knowledge *only* comes through objective observation. If one does not observe and experience something, then one cannot factually know it. If one has an idea or imagines something that one has never observed, it actually stems from a *similar* thing that the individual *has* observed. The new idea or imagined thing is only a copy, albeit faint and far removed, of the original.

Because of Hume's strict empiricism, he sought to remove the inquiries of metaphysics from philosophy. Metaphysics is a "division of philosophical study that is concerned with the fundamental nature of reality and being, and that includes ontology, cosmology, and often epistemology."[16] William Morris describes the philosopher thus:

> Hume's program for reform in philosophy thus has two related aspects: the elimination of metaphysics and the establishment of an empirical experimental science of human nature. He shifts the focus away from the traditional metaphysical search for "ultimate original principles" in order to concentrate on describing the "original principles" of human nature that we can discover through experience and observation, and to which we can give coherent cognitive content by tracing the ideas involved to the impressions that gave rise to them. He does so because claims to have found "ultimate principles" are not just

false, they are incoherent, because they go beyond anything that can be experienced.[17]

Hume placed knowledge in the firsthand experience of the objective observer. His distaste for metaphysics and insistence on the ability to observe all things also led him to denounce religion and all that goes with it as dangerous to the true pursuit of experience-based knowledge. In his irreverent essay, "The Natural History of Religion," Hume posits that religion began with ancient people creating gods to explain natural disasters. These primitive religions turn into polytheism and eventually monotheism. Monotheism leads to corruption and power struggles. Hume concludes that religion is bad for the world and only holds society back.[18]

Hume's contribution to the Rise of the Individual is in his emphasis on objective observation as the sole source of knowledge. To be known, something must be observed and experienced, as he states in *Enquiry Concerning the Principles of Morals.*

> Men are now cured of their passion for hypotheses and systems in natural philosophy, and will hearken to no arguments but those which are derived from experience. It is full time they should attempt a like reformation in all moral disquisitions; and reject every system of ethics, however subtle or ingenious, which is not founded on fact and observation.[19]

Hume started such reform. He inspired many thinkers, such as Charles Darwin, after him. Continuing where Locke's philosophy leaves off, Hume's work encourages questioning authority by doubting all that is not testable fact. He asserts that the individual should not assume that truths passed down through time are actually true, but, not taking them at face value, he should experience said truths himself. If that cannot be done, then no more time should be devoted to the pursuit of such a fruitless endeavor.

We can see how Jake has been influenced by Hume while at the same time going beyond Hume. The instructor rejects a metaphysical statement, something Hume would have agreed with, but Jake thinks he may have observed evidence to the contrary of the instructor's statement. Since Jake believes he has evidence for the spiritual world, he thinks the burden of proof is on the instructor to convince others that a spiritual world does not exist. Jake is not just going to take the instructor's word for it. His ranking of personal observation over and above authoritative statements is a move toward our next contributor, Søren Kierkegaard.

Søren Kierkegaard

While Jake's appearance may seem unusual to some, it is evidence that Jake is trying not to be like the crowd, even if the crowd is also trying to not be like the crowd. It is a form of his self-expression. This purposeful, outward self-expression can be traced back to Kierkegaard, who furthered the idea of questioning authority. He also took the persona of the individual and pushed it to the forefront. According to Kierkegaard, if Jake comes to the conclusion that a ghost lives in his guestroom and that conclusion affects how Jake lives, then it is true, regardless of what the authoritative scientific community may say about the situation.

Søren Kierkegaard spent most of his life (1813 to 1855) in Copenhagen, Denmark.[20] He was an author who wrote on many subjects, but he is best known for his philosophy and theology. William McDonald writes:

> Kierkegaard's central problematic was how to become a Christian in Christendom. The task was most difficult for the well-educated, since prevailing educational and cultural institutions tended to produce stereotyped members of "the crowd" rather than to allow individuals to discover their own unique identities.[21]

Kierkegaard was not looking for cookie-cutter Christians who were Christian because of societal norm. In order to facilitate this,

> Kierkegaard perceived a need to invent a form of communication which would not produce stereotyped identities. On the

contrary, he needed a form of rhetoric which would force people back onto their own resources, to take responsibility for their own existential choices, and to become who they are beyond their socially imposed identities.[22]

He did this by pressing people to question themselves and what they believed in order for them to "take individual responsibility for their claims about knowledge and value."[23]

While thinkers like Locke and Hume encouraged individuals to pursue objective knowledge—knowledge that is observable by all and therefore universal—Kierkegaard encouraged *subjective* knowledge instead. Subjective knowledge is that which is perceived by the individual alone and therefore does need not to be universal. Along with his subjective stance, Kierkegaard questioned why the individual believes something as true. By encouraging subjective questions about truth and life, Kierkegaard became known as the "Father of Existentialism." He emphasized the individual's contemplation of personal existence and choices.

In his *Concluding Unscientific Postscript*, Kierkegaard questions authority in his own way: he questioned the authority of objective, observable truth. Kierkegaard held that passion of belief and commitment to an idea are legitimate markers of truth for the individual, especially in the face of its uncertainty. This is in direct opposition to the untruth of "the crowd," which can be defined as "public opinion in the widest sense."[24] In other words, even though the crowd may have a certainty of knowledge in an objective sense, it is not true unless it is passionately believed by the individual.

The fact that Jake questions proof of spiritual things in direct opposition to his instructor shows how Jake has been influenced by the work of Kierkegaard. The impact of Kierkegaard's philosophy is clear in numerous choices he makes throughout his life, including the customization of his activities and appearance. Past philosophers' influence on Jake does not end with Kierkegaard, though. Next, we will see how Friedrich Nietzsche pushes Jake's rejection of the crowd to an extreme.

Friedrich Nietzsche

If Kierkegaard pushed the individual to the forefront, then Nietzsche put the individual high on a pedestal. Jake's refusal to be confined by marriage is a sign of Nietzsche's philosophy that conformity is for the weak. Nietzsche's position would be that getting married would be wrong for Jake and Loraine, when they already have what they want on their own terms. Nietzsche also opens up the possibility that they both could believe that a ghost lives in their guestroom, but they could each define "ghost" in different ways. Even in defining the ghost differently, though, they could agree that they are talking about the same ghost.

Friedrich Nietzsche was a German philosopher who lived from 1844 to 1900. If Kierkegaard was attempting to revitalize Christianity through philosophy, then Nietzsche would be his philosophical polar opposite. While launching from some of the same basic foundations as Kierkegaard, Nietzsche's atheist trajectory led him to similar but different conclusions for the individual.

Nietzsche came to a similar idea as Kierkegaard's "crowd." In the second essay in "On the Genealogy of Morals," he refers to people as herd animals sick with the repressive constraints of Christian morality:

> We modern men, we are the inheritors of thousands of years of vivisection of the conscience and self-inflicted animal torture. That's what we have had the longest practice doing, that is perhaps our artistry; in any case, it's something we have refined, the corruption of our taste. For too long man has looked at his natural inclinations with an "evil eye," so that finally in him they have become twinned with "bad conscience." An attempt to reverse this might, *in itself*, be possible—but who is strong enough for it, that is, to link as siblings bad conscience and the *unnatural* inclinations, all those aspirations for what lies beyond, those things which go against our senses, against our instincts, against nature, against animals—in short, the earlier ideals, all the ideals which are hostile to life, ideals of those who vilify the world?[25]

The conformity to societal norms was stifling the potential of the individual, but Nietzsche saw an existential hope: "the individual nevertheless has the potential to become something else, the sick animal is 'pregnant with a future.'"[26] For Nietzsche this meant following the individual's own will and carving out his purpose and existence according to his desires. Of course, what has to happen first is the deconstruction of what the "herd" considers authoritative truth.

Albeit for very different purposes, Kierkegaard and Nietzsche share the conclusion that, in order for an individual to live a life of truth, she must do it apart from, if not against, the community. While Kierkegaard focused on subjective truth, Nietzsche saw truth as a matter of perspective. He writes in *On the Genealogy of Morals*:

> The *only* seeing we have is seeing from a perspective; the *only* knowledge we have is knowledge from a perspective; and the *more* emotions we allow to be expressed in words concerning something, the *more* eyes, different eyes, we know how to train on the same thing, the more complete our "idea" of this thing, our "objectivity," will be.[27]

Perspectivism says that knowledge is always subject to individual interpretation. In other words, truth is variable. Nietzsche is not, however, saying that truth is *relative*, which is a misleading term that some people use today to describe the *absence* of truth. In the quotation above, he states that many different perspectives can paint a more complete picture. The more complete the picture, the closer we are to what is called "objective" truth. The idea that every unique perspective is necessary for the best understanding of truth further elevates the status of the Individual. An authoritative entity is not qualified to say what truth is—and could even cause harm by doing so. Assertions of truth from such entities lead to the sickness of the animals in the herd.

We can see how Jake has been affected by Nietzsche. His rejection of the societal norm of marriage illustrates his rejection of the herd. As Jake makes more decisions on his own, against the thought of authoritative entities, he becomes more free and healthy in Nietzsche's world. Nietzsche also allows Jake and Loraine to believe in their guestroom ghost; furthermore, they both can define "ghost" differently but still be right. In fact, the differing views of the guestroom ghost actually yield a better understanding of the ghost in whole.

Manifest Destiny

Manifest Destiny brings it all together for Jake. It embodies the ideas of the previous philosophers and amplifies them, with a uniquely American spin. Jake's appearance, his refusal to get married and be tied down to his girlfriend, his strained relationship with his father, his playing kickball, his being in a bluegrass band, his education, his chosen career, his selective agreement with his instructor's teaching, his many acquaintances but only being close to a few, among other aspects of his life—all of these things reveal his pursuing his dreams and aspirations as he sees fit. He does not allow anyone or anything to get in the way of how he wants his life to be. He is in the process of shaping his perfect world. Jake's way of perceiving the world is the result of Manifest Destiny.

Sixty-nine years after the United States declared its freedom from King George III, John L. O'Sullivan coined the term Manifest Destiny in order to describe the divine fate of the United States to spread westward through North America. Much of the driving force behind O'Sullivan's idea was the personal gain possible for those who tamed the Wild West. Wrapped up in the idea, as well—if not the basis of it—was the proposition in the United States' Declaration of Independence that every person (only white males at the time) has God-given rights to life, liberty, and the pursuit of happiness.[28]

O'Sullivan's credo clearly worked, and people moved west to grab their own piece of the divinely mandated fortune. As the United States expanded westward, pioneers discovered that people already were there, living freely and pursuing happiness. The pioneers did not see these indigenous people as having the same God-given rights as themselves, so the pioneers had no choice but to kill them or chase them off.

Although during the past fifty years,[29] some attention has been paid to the travesty of justice that occurred during that period, popular culture traditionally has glorified the pioneers and the United States' movement west.[30] At most, a cursory nod has been given to the poor treatment and slaughter of Native Americans, as well as animals such as American bison: it was unfortunate but at the same time necessary for progress to be made. All too often, the sentiment about these displaced peoples is that they were hurdles: they got in the way of the Manifest Destiny of brave individuals who, with great courage, sought life, liberty, and happiness in an emerging nation. Many people believe Western pioneers were brave heroes who simply did what had to be done.

The doctrine of Manifest Destiny has evolved during the past 160 years and represents different ideas to different people. I believe that a thorough study of the idea, its meaning, and its effects on American history would prove that it is ingrained in American culture. The independent, courageous pioneer is glorified as part of the cult of the individual. What has become woven into the fabric of American culture is that the individual is to pursue and protect his life, liberty, and happiness at all costs. These rights are God-given, after all, even if one does not believe in God. If someone or something gets in the way of these rights, the courageous recourse of the individual is to confront the obstacle head-on, remove it, and thereby prevent it from being an impediment to others. The people who live life in this manner are seen as heroic. Jake may not consciously see himself as a hero, but he would see anything that gets in the way of his Manifest Destiny as wrong and in need of removal.

Summary Analysis

We just took a wild, three hundred-year ride through history to examine the major contributors to our current individual-centric culture: a little from the pre-Enlightenment era, the Enlightenment, and the Modern movement. We can see how each philosopher influenced Jake and how these advances in thought have shaped us, too, in ways we probably had not noticed. John Locke developed a philosophy of individual observation of the world to confirm or deny what has been disseminated as knowledge from authoritative entities. He wanted the individual to think for himself. Such notions led to his insistence on objective observation for the individual. Combining that with the idea of *tabula rasa,* or blank slate, he set the stage for establishing the modern empirical method.

Locke also advanced a concept of how the individual relates to the world, as well as how the world relates to the individual. All of Locke's philosophies are steeped in his worldview that God created the world and gave humans a "natural law" by which to live; therefore, his concept of the individual is one that has God-given rights to life, health, liberty, and possessions. He also rejected the British king in favor of more individual freedom.

Basic impact of Locke today:

- Authority should be questioned.
- Individuals should reason out truth for themselves through observation and experience.
- Humans have individual and equal God-given rights to life, health, and possessions.

David Hume catapulted off of Locke's individual observation and championed the idea of objective knowledge. According to Hume, true knowledge is observable and able to be verified (experienced). Knowledge is objective only if it is not contaminated with the bias of the individual observer. In other words, any rational person can observe and experience the same truth if it is truly objective. He also was concerned that too much time was wasted on "airy" sciences that could not be proven. The pursuit of knowledge for Hume was concrete and objective: anything that appeared to fall outside those boundaries needed to conform to them if such a thing was going to be taken seriously.

Basic impact of Hume today:

- Truth is universally verifiable through observation and experience.
- Knowledge such as that found in religious beliefs is not verifiable or scientific, and objective knowledge therefore supersedes it.

In a sort of philosophical backlash, Søren Kierkegaard placed knowledge on the subjective experience of the individual. What mattered for him was passion. Any knowledge that is taken for granted by the "crowd" is to be questioned on a journey of self-discovery to see whether such knowledge is true for the individual. Kierkegaard wanted individuals to break free from the mold of the crowd, questioning and contemplating their own existence and beliefs apart from the influence of the crowd or the directives of authoritarian entities.

Basic impact of Kierkegaard today:

- Question authority, as well as popular opinion or thought, at all times.
- The individual's passionate belief in something makes it true knowledge.
- Subjectivity and "why" for the individual is more important than objectivity and "how."

Picking up where Kierkegaard left off, albeit in a distinctly antireligious fashion, Friedrich Nietzsche pushed the idea of subjectivity even farther in his attempts to free the individual from the "herd." In order for the individual to reach her full potential apart from the herd and to be cured of the sickness of conformity, she must follow her own desire at every move, lest an outside force mold her to gain power.

Not to be forgotten is Nietzsche's views on the acquisition of knowledge. Knowledge is about perspective: the individual interprets everything in a way that is subjectively unique. The individual's perspective of truth is one of many, and, when the many are taken in whole, they create a fuller understanding of the actual truth.

Basic impact of Nietzsche today:

- Conformity to a standard is a sign of weakness of the individual.
- Every individual's point of view is a valid view of a truth.
- One needs to follow every personal desire in order to be a free individual.

On the basis of John Locke's definition of the equality of individuals, the idea of Manifest Destiny was ingrained in the American West. It resulted in the glorification of pioneers in pursuit of life, liberty, and happiness. The pursuit is God-given, and anything that gets in the way needs to be removed. Many view the individuals who tamed the West as brave and courageous.

Basic impact of Manifest Destiny today:

- The individual has the right to pursue being an individual by force.
- Individuals form their own definitions of "life, liberty, and the pursuit of happiness."
- The primary directive for the individual is the quest for the self-defined "life, liberty, and the pursuit of happiness."
- The doctrine of Individualism is a result of that quest.

Observing the summary sections, we see that Jake is not an exception but that he has elements of his life in common with others in the West. These traits were not always part of society; the philosophers discussed were innovators of their time. The way they thought and the philosophies that they proposed were not the norm in the societies in which they lived. During the past three hundred years, the status of the Individual has risen steadily, and this elevation affects the way people in the West interact and view the world today.

What has occurred is radicalized individualization. Without a conscious understanding that these thought processes have been taught to us by our culture over time, the individual passionately believes (as Kierkegaard would assert) that all of his assumptions, ideas, and core values are individual and self-chosen. Everything is internalized. He is his own man. He will make his own choices and decisions. Everything he believes to be true, he discovered[31] to be true. Everything he believes to be false, he discovered to be false. He has a right to his perspective of the world and how he defines life, liberty, and the pursuit of happiness ("Divine Dream"[32]), and nothing outside of him has a right to get in the way of his living that out.[33]

We observe that this radical individualization includes an inherited suspicion of authoritative entities, conformity, and popular opinion. As a result, the individual has a suspicion (often subconscious) of any community of people with surface-level, built-in assumptions, ideas, and core values. The suspicion occurs because any outside influence must be questioned: what does the outside influence gain by the conformity of the individual? How do the assumptions, ideas, and core values of the outside influence go with or against the individual's pursuit of the Divine Dream?

To give an example of the individual's suspicion of surface-level, built-in assumptions, ideas, and core values we will take a look at a night in the life of Jake. If you recall, Jake likes nothing more than to go the corner bar with his friends to drink cheap beer and shoot pool.

> One day, one of his friends says that he has always wanted to check out the Elk Lodge that is a couple of blocks away. His friend passes the mysterious building and its neon Hamm's Beer sign almost every day, and the curiosity of it is getting the better of him. On a lark, Jake and his friend decide to check it out that Saturday night.

They suspiciously enter the building and notice that much is strange about the Elk Lodge: some odd but intriguing decorations, some weird pamphlets that neither of them has ever seen before, and pictures of a bunch of kids in hospital beds. They have come this far, though, and it should make for a good story back at the bar. They press on.

While a few things are strange, much of it is familiar to them, as well. In fact, they both feel oddly at home because, in the dark, stale air, they see several guys bellied up to long bar, talking and laughing loudly. Two well-kept pool tables are prominent in the room, as the lights above them cut them out of the dark like stars on stage. Jake and his friend look at each other and smile. Jake heads to the closest pool table to mark their place in line with a quarter, while his friend goes over to the bar to order a couple of beers.

After several hours of carousing with the guys at the lodge, Jake tells one of them that their newfound hangout is "awesome!" Jake wonders out loud why more people aren't hanging out here. The fellow next to him explains that Saturdays are open nights, but normally guys need to be members of the Lodge to use the facilities. Jake looks at the pristine pool tables, and, having won two games in a row and being more than a little drunk, he jokingly asks what it takes to be a member.

The Lodge member brightens up and says, "We are always looking for more members! Jake, you and Leo would fit in great! Technically, to be members you have to agree to follow the rules that are written up there on the wall behind the bar."

Jake strains to see the sign in the dark, when the Lodge member says "Look, basically all you really have to do is love to drink beer, shoot pool, and help sick kids in the hospital."

Check, check . . . whoa! Jake loves to drink beer and shoot pool, but what's with all this helping kids stuff? Why should he *have* to do that? Can't he just come and hang out? What exactly is going here at the Elk Lodge anyway? He knew something was strange about this place.

Jake's suspicion of the Elk Lodge is immediately rekindled once he is made aware of the Lodge's core values, even though he agrees with two of the three. Any connection that he made with the Elk Lodge is quickly eroded by the overtness of its values. His initial reaction is distrust when an outside force requires him to conform to a value that he has not yet accepted. He is not necessarily against helping kids in the hospital, but he has not come to that conclusion on his own yet; therefore, his immediate reaction, when directly confronted with the idea from an outside community, is suspicion and rejection.

This perception of individuality is what drives the personal identity of most people in the West. For some it is conscious, but for most it is subconscious. The problem with this perception of individuality is that we are not individuals purely of our own making. We are always creatures of community being influenced and shaped by outside forces. No person in contact with another person exists in a vacuum. The use of language itself illustrates that phenomenon.[34] In other words, for an individual to be truly a self-made, self-chosen person is impossible. The sense of individuality is not *completely* unfounded, however, because the individual has the ability to choose many of the communities of which he is part.[35]

Jake's life also illustrates another phenomenon of the Rise of the Individual: by constantly challenging the authority of community, the desires of the individual significantly reduced the role of community as understood before the Enlightenment. Jake touches many different communities and has a ton of acquaintances through social media, yet he only really knows and talks to a few people. Jake doesn't know how to be part of a community. He has a hard time seeing communities beyond what he gets out of them; he is the star of his movie, after all. Jake is not alone in this phenomenon: most people in the Americanized West have lost the ability to *be* part of a community. They just know how to take part in a community.

We could spend an entire book discussing the history of individualism, but we have suitably observed that the Rise of the Individual in the West has conflicted with the idea of community during the past three hundred years. After some honest observation and introspection, we can see the characteristics of such individualism in ourselves. It is one of the fruits of Modernism. By now, most people reading this likely have already heard rumblings that we now have entered a new era. Many arguments occur about what exactly to call it—Postmodern, Modern-Modern, post-Enlightenment, post-Christian, or some other label. What we call it is not of the utmost importance. What is important is the recognition that this transition era has had an effect on community and the individual.

Part Two:
The Transition from Modern Thought

I recently spoke on this topic to a room full of people whose ages varied. When I brought up Facebook, something intriguing occurred. Some people in the room felt the need to voice their opinions about Facebook—namely, that it is stupid and pointless. After some time, we moved on to a different topic when suddenly, like a runaway grocery cart in a parking lot, the stupidity of Facebook was brought back into the conversation. This happened several times, and eventually others in the group starting coming to the defense of Facebook, saying that it is a flawed but helpful tool.

Thinking back on the oddness of that day, I tried to analyze what happened and whether I should ever mention Facebook in public again. I came to the conclusion that the repeated deviation from the topic I was presenting was actually a sign that we are in a transitional era of thought.[36] Most of the Facebook naysayers were older than fifty years of age, while those in favor of Facebook tended to be in their early to mid-twenties. The groups were not hard and fast; in fact, a few people in the fifty-plus group were pro-Facebook. One would expect such disparity when trying to identify groups as Modern or Postmodern. While generational lines can be a good indicator, they are not definitive because "Modern" and "Postmodern" label ways of thinking and therefore are informed by much more than age alone. (I am not suggesting that using Facebook represents Postmodern thinking or behavior or *vice versa*: a lot of "Moderns" use

Facebook, while a lot of "Postmoderns" do not. What I am saying is that it can be a good illustration of this transitional era of thought.)

I prefer to think of our current state of thought as transitional rather than define it as purely Postmodern. I liken this era to a Modern Hangover.[37] The West has been on a three-day bender with Modernism, pushing it to its limits. As the West became more intoxicated with Modern thought, Modern thought became more euphoric and promising. Imagining life without Modernism became difficult. Now morning has dawned, and the general populace has a wicked headache and some regrets about what happened the night before, when it was under the strong influence of Modernism. Lessons have been learned, and we are cautious about Modern thought; however, in the end we are still hooked on Modernism. In general, we push back against Modernism and try to move past it. We are addicted, though, and everything we do is tainted by it.[38] In the end, we have yet to see what Postmodernism actually is, as we are in a transitional era from Modernism to Postmodernism.

With the spread of this transitional era came the newly recognized need for community in the life of the individual—a reaction against the diminished role of community in Modernism. Individualism naturally leads to isolation of the individual. Community, however, is necessary for the individual to express his interests, beliefs, values, and goals. We are creatures built for community. Modernism creates an unsatisfactory balance between individual and community. This dissatisfaction is one of the regrets of our "Modern hangover." As a result, the importance of community has been elevated once again in Western society. As observers of our culture, we could realistically say that this reintroduction is owing to the false sense of individuality collapsing on itself: people want more out of life than their self-defined pursuit of individual happiness can provide.

Since we are in the Modern Hangover and individualism is all we know, however, we create community in a very Modern, individual-centric way. Social media websites and texting are examples of attempts at community in the transition era. These venues provide a sense of community, but in an individualistic manner. Relative anonymity and a lack of accountability allow the individual to dictate and filter everything that the community knows about him. He can also drop in or drop out whenever he pleases, thus making community more consumable for the individual. We in the West are community consumers. Community can be more than that, but only if the individual chooses it to be so. The terms of engagement take place on the individual's terms.

I may seem to be tearing down these venues. I am not; I am only attempting to illustrate how these venues of community are still peppered with the individualism inherited from the past three hundred years. I believe that the transitional era in which we find ourselves offers hope. The desire for community is important. We are creatures built for community, both with each other and with God.[39] The transition of thought from Modernism to a new era offers more positives than just the rise of community: the reaffirmation of the spiritual world, openness to discussing opposing views, and the recognition that sometimes the here-and-now consequences of sin need to be faced rather than ignored.

Now that we have observed the Rise of the Individual, as well as the newly recognized need for community, we are able to delve into how that plays out in our culture today. Our observation will help us understand both how and why people act the way they do in communities. This insight is beneficial not only when dealing with others but also when considering our own actions. It is time to dive into the Fluid Confluence of Communities.

Part Three:
The Fluid Confluence of Communities

The beginning of this endeavor began with a description of Milwaukee being founded at a confluence. If you recall, a confluence is the meeting place of two or more streams. Now, instead of the three rivers coming together in Milwaukee, picture a grand Confluence where many streams come together into a massive river that is so wide that one cannot see one river bank from the other. The streams that contribute to this Confluence originate from distant and varied lands; therefore, each adds unique water to the Confluence, with differing temperatures, minerals, and organisms. If one were to take a sample of the water in the Confluence in a particular spot and test its makeup, that sample would differ from a sample at every other spot in the Confluence. The Confluence is vast and ever-changing with new streams developing and working their way to join the Confluence every day. Such is the Fluid Confluence of Communities in which we are living.

We have observed that people today have recognized the need for community in their lives. Since community is not built into our society because of the Rise of the Individual, individuals are left to search out community for themselves. People are fulfilling their need for community, and technology has enabled worldwide communication and selection of these communities. Because of worldwide communication, our society has become globalized, and one need not travel far to have a smorgasbord of choices of community. The communities of the world are streaming together into one vast Confluence of Communities.

The Confluence may appear to exist in a virtual world because much of its substance comes from global communication. Technology and worldwide communication, however, also have given the individual the ability to identify and meet local people who share that individual's specific community needs. An example of this is my love of cyclocross racing.

> For many, cyclocross is a nonsense word, so allow me to give a brief description. Cyclocross is a form of bicycle racing that normally takes place in early fall and midwinter. Bicycles used for the sport have the look of road bikes (think ten-speed bike) but are stronger and have a few modifications that allow riding in grass, mud, gravel, sand, and snow. Different brakes and wider tires with knobs are the most notable modifications. The races normally take place in parks and involve about 1.75-mile laps that includes cross-country terrain and one or two sections in which riders must dismount the bicycle and carry it over an obstacle, then remount the bicycle as fast as possible.

> Using the internet, I am able to watch races from all over the world. I can track results and get race reports from even the smallest local races thousands of miles from my home. I know how friends' races went at their local scene. I can learn about and compare all the technology and parts that go into a cyclocross bike, from the early history of the sport to the cutting edge of the future. After a little time spent online, anyone with a little knowledge of bicycles can easily become a competent member of the cyclocross community.

> I was able to find out what was happening in my local scene before I even moved to the state. Once we moved to our current location and the cyclocross season came around, I easily found out where and when practices were being held, as well as venues for local races. I may not have known anyone personally at my first few races, but the community outsider never would have

known that. In fact, most community insiders would never have guessed I was new to the scene, either.[40]

On one side of the spectrum, my description of cyclocross is intriguing enough for some folks that they are going to put down this book and hop online right now to actually check it out for themselves. On the other hand, some would say that it sounds like a complete waste of time and energy for adults who like to play with oversized children's toys. Others may land anywhere in between these two extremes. Such individual community preference makes the Confluence fluid.

While we are in a transition era that recognizes the need for community, we are still, as we have observed, living in a society that prioritizes the individual above all things. Prioritization of the individual has spurred on the fluid customization of communities. People seek out community, but often in a narcissistic fashion. Pursuing one's definition of the Divine Dream, one picks and chooses parts of countless communities as one sees fit in an ever-changing Confluence.

One looks inward, forming one's identity out of one's choices and desires, and then attempts to mold a community around that identity. Once the availability of choice and the ingrained cultural perception of the individual are combined, what happens is assimilation, and even subjugation, to the attractive aspects of new, chosen communities, while at the same time the dismissal of some aspects of those chosen communities. I believe that this customization is largely done subconsciously. After that wordy description, customization of communities may seem like an overly complex idea, so we will take some time to look at a real-world example to observe how this happens.

Customization of communities is an area in which the fallacy of stark individualism looms large. The individual can choose in which communities she is inclined to take part. She enters a new, chosen community, then customizes her participation in it according to her individual desires. The desires to which she customizes the new community are not her subjective desires alone, however: they have been shaped and influenced by all of the

30

previous communities of which she has already been part. Even her choice of new communities is partly informed and influenced by her previous communities.

Nancy's story might make this clearer:

> Nancy is 30 years old, is single, and works as a bank teller. Her job pays the bills, and that is good enough for her; she doesn't have any real aspirations to move up in the company. Nancy has a few work friends. These are the few people that she eats lunch with and sits next to in meetings. She doesn't hang out with them outside of work, however, and she avoids conversations that get too personal at work. Besides being a bit bored at times, she generally is happy with her work situation. When she punches out she doesn't think about the bank or the people there until she has to show up the next day.
>
> What does occupy her mind when she isn't working (and often when she is working, too) is kayaking. Nancy loves to kayak and even races on Sunday mornings. Through the years of paddling, racing, and visiting the store where she buys her kayak equipment, she has made some good friends in the sport. When Nancy wants to be with people, she seeks out her kayaking friends. She feels most comfortable when she is around them because they just seem to understand her.
>
> A lot of her kayaking friends are vegetarian or vegan. After hearing about the benefits of a vegetarian diet from her friends, she decides to adopt the lifestyle. One thing that convinced her was that many of her friends had been beating her in races. She's not personally against eating animals—after all, she used to bow hunt with her dad when she was younger and still has fond memories of it. The issue for her is a healthy lifestyle.
>
> Her relationship with her dad isn't so great these days, though. When she goes to his house for dinner, meat is always served. Her father takes her refusal to eat meat as more of her rebellion

31

against her upbringing, especially the family's Catholic faith. She stopped going to Mass in high school after her mom died of breast cancer. As far as she is concerned, Catholicism is a waste of time for confused people. She feels closer to God on the water in her kayak than she ever did while sitting in a church pew. She knows her dad is a devout Catholic and worries about her, but he shouldn't: she and God are just fine.

Although she thinks Jesus was just a great man who was misunderstood, she wears a gold cross necklace that was a gift from her mother. Fond memories are attached to it, not to mention the fact that it is pretty and fashionable. (Nancy enjoys keeping up to date with fashion and celebrity news.)

In the example Nancy chooses to become vegetarian. She may attribute the decision to her individual subjective desire—and on the surface it appears to be so—yet, if we deconstruct the decision, we observe that is far from a choice that she made on her own.

Nancy becomes part of the kayaking community, and it becomes an important aspect of her identity. Over time, she accepts many of the assumptions, ideas, and core values of the kayaking community. She befriends people in the kayaking community who share many of her assumptions, ideas, and core values.

As these relationships strengthen, so does her trust of these friends, many of whom are vegetarian. She is therefore introduced to the vegetarian community through the kayaking community. She joins the vegetarian community because of one main assumption of that community—that is, that vegetarianism represents a healthy lifestyle. Nancy is willing to subject herself to that assumption because she hopes it will benefit her in the kayaking community, of which she is already a part. At the same time, she rejects the idea that killing and eating animals is wrong because of a value she was given when she was younger.

The example of Nancy's place in the Confluence could go on for a long time and be scrupulously detailed. In her example's simplicity, though, some of the streams of community clearly come together in the spot where Nancy is wading in the Confluence. Nancy's example highlights for us what we have observed so far—that people today identify themselves within a Fluid Confluence of Communities. They do this mostly subconsciously, as a result of the prioritization of the individual borne of the Enlightenment and Modernism; the recognized need of community in our current transition era; and the ability to pick and choose aspects of various communities. Many people would describe the spot where they are wading in the Fluid Confluence as their own "community."

In Nancy's example we observe that she is wading in the Confluence at a spot where one of her subcommunities is a group of kayakers. She most closely identifies with those kayakers who race; who are vegetarian for health reasons; who believe in god; who were raised Catholic but are not anymore; who enjoy some celebrity gossip; and who work 9-to-5, white-collar jobs to pay the bills. The more someone fits those characteristics, the more Nancy sees that person as part of her "community."

Every person in the Confluence has her own nuanced version of a perfect community. Even with the simplified version of Nancy's life, imagining her finding a sizable group of people with whom she wholeheartedly identifies would be difficult. More likely, some people do not fit the mold she has created for herself, yet, because they do share some interest, belief, value, background, or goal, they find themselves sharing the same subcommunity at times.

Any person who shares aspects of Nancy's community is going to have his own spot in the Confluence, and his "community" is going to differ from Nancy's "community." As he pursues his definition of the Divine Dream, he picks and chooses parts of countless communities as he sees fit in an ever-changing Confluence. Subcommunities are shared, but every person's self-defined community is unique.

The final thing we observe in the Fluid Confluence of Communities is the existence of islands. Not everyone is treading water. Some individuals are standing on or grasping hold of dry ground. An island exists for the individual because he allows a certain community to influence him openly in defining how he interacts with other communities in the Confluence. He readily accepts this influence. We can see how this is a departure from his normal participation in the Confluence. This is an important concept, and we will thoroughly discuss several types of islands later in the book.

The Fluid Confluence of Communities is not necessarily a good or bad thing: it is just a reality that will not change dramatically any time soon. Observing how it works enables us to see how it affects our lives and the lives of those around us. Our observations give us insights as to why people perceive the world the way they do. As I will illustrate later, understanding how we perceive the world is crucial to how we engage it. Some of the opportunities that the Confluence affords will be addressed later, but for now let us take a look at a few of its complications.

Complications

Communication

The individualization found in community is not always on a surface level; in fact, it is much deeper. This can create a serious disconnect in communication. When two or more people share aspects of one community but are not wading in the exact same part of the Confluence, a false assumption often is made that they are all on the same page and in agreement about the definition of the pursuit of the Divine Dream. In other words, two people are unlikely to view the world in the exact same way unless they are in the exact same part of the Confluence. Take the example of Nancy again:

> One Thursday evening Nancy is out to eat at one of her favorite vegetarian restaurants by herself. As she is eating, she notices a man walking around from table to table handing out flyers and talking to the people eating. She is curious about what he is doing as he makes his way to her side of the restaurant. Seeing Nancy look at him the man makes eye contact and seizes the opportunity to grab the empty chair at the other end of her table.

"May I?," he blurts out quickly as he sits down. He slides a flyer over to Nancy, an advertisement for a protest that is going to take place at the meatpacking factory just outside of town. Before Nancy has a chance to speak, he says, "It is time for those bastards to learn that they can't profit off the death of innocent animals anymore. There are enough people like us living here now that we can tell them we don't want them here anymore, and they are going to have to listen!"

Nancy is taken aback. Why would this vulgar guy just assume she agrees with him about protesting? She's here because she loves the asparagus risotto, not because she is some sort of PETA crusader!

The protestor assumes that, because Nancy is in a vegetarian restaurant, she shares his views on the treatment of animals and his ideas of how to live out that value. We already established that Nancy is vegetarian for health reasons and has no moral objection to people killing and eating animals. Miscommunication based on assumptions happens regularly in the Fluid Confluence. A little bit of recollection should turn up a least a few examples of this occurring in most people's lives.

The assumptions made by people in shared communities have consequences both within and outside the Church. Within in the Church, miscommunication happens regularly and often goes unnoticed. How often are teachers and preachers talking past people in the Church by using terms and concepts that the people do not know or understand? People then do not speak up or ask questions because they sense that others assume that they already should know what various church-related terms and concepts mean. Potentially worse is the possibility that people in the Church define terms their own way and then apply their own definitions when they hear preachers and teachers speak. Everyone assumes they are in agreement but in reality that couldn't be farther from the truth.

Once we observe that we are all in the Fluid Confluence of Communities, we can recognize the need for thorough communication. Because of the

Confluence, relaying information is highly nuanced. For example, one cannot simply assume that others define "sin" the same way. If one is going to use the term "sin," one must first establish what one understands it to mean, as well as find out what the other person understands it to mean. It is as though we are in a foreign land trying to communicate with local citizens. This work may sound exhausting and counterproductive; however, thorough communication is a necessity when so many people innately question outside sources and when self-definition is both the right and goal of life.[41] If we want communication to be fruitful—fully achieving our intended goals—then we must be thorough.

Identity

The Confluence reinforces the post-Enlightenment Western worldview that identity for the individual is internal and trumps allegiance to any one entity. We traced the roots of Modern individualism that dictate that the individual is to be objective and taught to question authority. Oddly enough, the result of individualism is subjectivism and self-definition, which the Confluence feeds. As the individual tailors her "community" to her own desires via customization, she begins to find her identity in that tailored community. As she wades through the Confluence, the communities in which she chooses to take part can become more of a reflection of her personal identity. She will also tend to avoid communities that challenge her personal identity. Since she is taking part in numerous subcommunities, she can easily distance herself from one—if that one changes or asks for too much commitment—and move toward another that has not changed or does not require as much allegiance.

If any community that is not an island requires her to be any person other than the person she chooses[42] to be, then her suspicion of that community will rise, and she will distance herself from it in order not to lose power—an illustration of the narcissism associated with customizing communities in the Confluence. Community ultimately is consumable and is used to feed the purposes of the individual. If it no longer does this, the person wades to another spot in the Confluence where she feels as though her identity is not being shaped by an outside force.[43]

Here is how Nancy's story illustrates this:

> While packing up after kayaking, Nancy overhears that some of her friends are going to the protest at the meat-packing company. On hearing the news she hastens her work and avoids eye contact with the friends who are protesting. The last thing she needs now, after the incident at the restaurant, is for one of her *friends* to come after her with that animal-rights stuff.
>
> She gets most of her equipment into the car when Jill, a friend and a protestor, approaches and says, "So, Nance, we will see you on Monday in front of Meyers Packing, right?"
>
> Wishing she had packed faster in order to avoid this conversation, Nancy plays dumb. "Why? What's going on?"
>
> "We are going to let them know that they can't profit off of the death of innocent animals anymore."
>
> Still packing, Nancy responds, "Aw, you guys know me. It's not about animals with me; I just want to be healthy."
>
> With a bit of irritation in her voice, Jill quips, "Come on, Nance. You have been off that stuff long enough to realize that there is no need to hurt any living creature in order for us to survive! It's not *just* about being healthy."
>
> She is finally fully packed, and as she gets into the car, Nancy smiles and says, "I'll think about it." Driving away, Nancy's mind floods with arguments about why she shouldn't have to protest the supposed cruelty to animals. She starts to rethink being vegetarian. It isn't like she has won any races since she has become one. She then starts to wonder what walking away

from vegetarianism would mean for her comfort level at the kayaking scene. She has a lot to figure out.

When Nancy's internal identity is challenged by an outside influence, she questions her allegiance to that community. She finds herself in the same place as Jake at the Elk Lodge. Her suspicion occurs because the community is asking her to do something or be someone outside her comfort level. As she recognizes this, she questions the outside influence: what do her vegetarian friends, or the vegetarian cause, gain by her conforming to their standards? How do the assumptions, ideas, and core values of the outside influence go with or against the individual's pursuit of the Divine Dream? In other words, will Nancy still be the Nancy she wants to be if she chooses to submit to their assumptions, ideas, and core values?

Highlighting the complication of internal identity in the Confluence accentuates an issue with the individual's pursuit of the Divine Dream. As she personalizes her "community" around her desires, she can become the god in her life. Anything that challenges her perception of how the world works can simply be removed from her life since she believes that she is the standard everything must be measured against. In other words, narcissistic customization can be a form of idolatry, and the Fluid Confluence of Communities can easily feed our desire to follow other gods.

Compartmentalization

Although the Confluence has allowed people to bring multiple communities together into their "community," it also enables the compartmentalization of those communities. Compartmentalization is the segmentation and separation of the activities, beliefs, and communities in one's life. The borders between these compartments often are hard and fast, creating a separation that is not to be traversed. Often the thought of mixing the separated compartments is seen as nonnegotiable. A notable example of nonnegotiable compartmentalization is the separation of faith communities from secular communities in Western society.[44] Pro-abortion Catholics are an example of compartmentalization.

In Nancy's story, we can see how she might compartmentalize three communities in her life: her job and work relationships, kayaking, and family life. These communities do not mingle for Nancy. They are separate, and the idea of them mixing never crosses Nancy's mind. In fact, the very thought of them mixing makes her anxious. She does not talk about kayaking with her work friends, and she certainly doesn't want her father showing up at the bank.

At first glance, compartmentalization may not seem like a drawback; however, it can cause complications. One problem is that, when compartmentalization is combined with the ease of consumer-based customization of communities, the individual can feel isolated. When the subcommunities of a person's life are distinct from each other, removing or adding a community, without feeling any ripples in one's other communities, is easy to do.

Nancy, for example, could switch jobs, and her kayaking friends may never know it. She *may* choose to let her kayaking friends know about doing so, thereby letting the communities mingle. She could also instead continue to keep the two communities compartmentalized and deal with the major life change alone, without the knowledge or support of her closest friends. Because of compartmentalization, many people who take part in numerous communities, and who often are around others, can feel isolated and alone.

Another difficulty with compartmentalization is that it reinforces the complications of communication and identity. Compartmentalization can enhance barriers that block thorough and fruitful communication. In the case of personal identity, compartmentalization allows one to distance oneself from a community that may seem suspicious.

Summary of the Fluid Confluence of Communities

The Fluid Confluence of Communities is the direct result of the Rise of the Individual, the renewed recognition of the need for community, and today's technology and ease of worldwide communication. The Confluence allows people to take part in communities that would not have been possible even fifty years ago. It enables individuals to customize their "community" around their personal definition of the pursuit of the Divine Dream. In the resulting Confluence, community often is a consumable used by the individual.

The Confluence is fluid and ever-changing as new streams of community develop and join. Individuals wade from spot to spot in the Confluence seeking out community to fulfill their desire. Along the way, they fine-tune their participation in every community as they see fit. Some even grab hold of an island. For two individuals to define the Divine Dream the exact same way, they would need to be wading in the exact same spot of the Confluence.

The customization of communities in the Confluence creates some complications, including communication challenges. One cannot simply assume that because another person shares one's community that that person defines or sees the world in the same way. In fact, the two could have divergent ways of seeing the world; therefore, communication must be thorough, with both parties defining things as they go, in order for it to be fruitful.

Another complication is the Confluence's reinforcement of the Western idea that personal identity is self-generated and therefore internal. Once again, having highly customized communities feeds the narcissism of the individual: it is his right to pursue the Divine Dream in the way he sees fit, and no outside source has the right to influence that pursuit. To influence that pursuit would be to try to control who he is and how he sees himself.

Compartmentalization is the last complication—often a complication-intensifier, rather than a stand-alone issue. By creating separation of communities, compartmentalization feeds and supports the other complications, thereby allowing a sense of isolation. It can impede Christians from serving freely, as we will discuss later.

Now that we have established the Fluid Confluence of Communities, we can begin addressing some of the questions raised in the introduction: What is the role of the Church in the Confluence? How should Christians behave in the Confluence? How do we effectively share the Gospel in the Confluence? We will begin with the role of the Church in the Confluence. In order to establish the role of the Church, we need to observe some more history.

Part Four:
The Kingdom Community

The Rise of the King

Take some time to read the first three chapters of Genesis, then put the Scriptures down and come back here.[45] In the first and second chapters of Genesis, God defines life for Adam and Eve; who they are in relation to God (Genesis 1:26); who they are in relation to creation (1:26); their personal identities (1:27, 2:25); their vocations (1:28); what they are to eat (1:29); and their relationship to each other (2:18, 24). All the major categories are covered.

In the third chapter, Satan tempts them, and their sin of wanting to be like God results in the corruption of everything God had initially laid out for them (3:16-24). Sin did not remove the definition of life that God gave them, but, because of sin, people no longer would be able to live life in the way God originally defined it. Instead, people would start living life more on their own terms, choosing not to walk after God's ways but in their own sinful ways. All was not lost, though—hope remained. God promises to crush Satan and the curse of sin in time (3:15).

Fast-forward through history a bit, and God is so fed up with the rank odor of sin coming from the planet that He washes it clean with a flood. Noah actually walked after God's ways and attempted to live life as God defined, so

He saves a few people to repopulate the Earth. In doing so, God tweaks His definition of life a bit by changing the dietary restrictions (Genesis 9:1-5).

Fast-forward again, and we see the first sign that the plan to crush Satan and sin are being put into motion (Genesis 12:1-3). God promises Abram (soon to be Abraham) that, if he has faith in His promise, God will make Abraham's descendants too numerous to count and that, through them, all people will be blessed. Move forward in history again to the Israelites—the blood descendants of Abraham—and we see how God keeps His promise when He redeems them from slavery in Egypt. He says to the Israelites that, because of this redemption, "I will be your God, and you will be my people" (Exodus 6:6-7).

God leads them to Mount Sinai and gives them detailed instructions on how to live in relation to Himself, to each other, and to creation.[46] He defines the "groove" for them.[47] The Levitical laws show how God defined life at that time. The more closely one adhered to God's definition of life, the more seamless, or "in the groove," one's life would be.

> And if you faithfully obey the voice of the Lord your God, being careful to do all His commandments that I command you today, the Lord your God will set you high above all the nations of the earth. And all these blessings shall come on you and overtake you, if you obey the voice of the Lord your God. Blessed shall you be in the city, and blessed shall you be in the field. Blessed shall be the fruit of your womb and the fruit of your ground and the fruit of your cattle, the increase of your herds and the young of your flock. Blessed shall be your basket and your kneading bowl. Blessed shall you be when you come in, and blessed shall you be when you go out. [48]

Notice how the Exodus illustrates that the Israelites were a people chosen and redeemed by God *before* they were given any commandments as how to live—further indication that God's redemption, not the commandments, make the Israelites God's people. Defining life was done in order to show the Israelites how to live in the groove as His people, something they had lost or never known.

His people eventually rejected having Him as their King; they wanted an earthly king like other nations. God gave them what they wanted, and it did not go well. Many of Israel's kings chased after other gods. The nation was torn and divided. A few times the rebellion progressed to the point at which the people did not really know God at all anymore, and they certainly were not living in the groove. God was always faithful to His promises, though, and sent prophets to tell the people to repent and turn back to Him. The prophets reminded the people of the promise of God to crush Satan and sin found in Genesis 3:15. God would do this through a King unlike any in Israel's history. This King would redeem them once and for all and fulfill the promise made to Abraham, thereby fulfilling the promise made in the Garden to Adam and Eve. The promised King would restore the people of Israel to God's good grace and lead them in peace forever.

> For to us a child is born,
>> to us a son is given;
>>> and the government shall be upon His shoulder,
>> and His name shall be called
>>> Wonderful Counselor, Mighty God,
>>> Everlasting Father, Prince of Peace.
> Of the increase of His government and of peace
>> there will be no end,
>>> on the throne of David and over His kingdom,
>> to establish it and to uphold it
>>> with justice and with righteousness
>> from this time forth and forevermore.
>>> The zeal of the LORD of hosts will do this. [49]

And:

> Behold, a king will reign in righteousness,
>> and princes will rule in justice.

Each will be like a hiding place from the wind,
a shelter from the storm,
like streams of water in a dry place,
like the shade of a great rock in a weary land.
Then the eyes of those who see will not be closed,
and the ears of those who hear will give attention.
The heart of the hasty will understand and know,
and the tongue of the stammerers will hasten to speak
distinctly.
The fool will no more be called noble,
nor the scoundrel said to be honorable. [50]

The faithful people of the Old Testament looked forward to this King, to the coming Messiah.[51] They were looking for the restoration of their nation. They awaited the One that would "sit at the right hand of Yahweh" and rule all of creation (Psalm 110)—a King to usher in the Kingdom of God, uniting them and leading them in living life the way God defined it (Isaiah 2:2-5).

About 2,000 years after the promise was made to Abraham, Jesus of Nazareth was born. He is the One who fulfilled the promise that was made in Genesis 3:15, the One who would crush Satan and sin, the Messiah and King for whom the faithful had been waiting. Jesus actually was more than what they had anticipated or expected. He began His public work, "proclaiming the gospel of God, and saying, 'The time is fulfilled, and the kingdom of God is at hand; repent and believe in the gospel.'"[52]

The faithful of Israel had been waiting for this good news, and they took Jesus to be a prophet. He was announcing that it was time to turn from doing things their own way and turn back to God because He was going to restore the kingdom.[53] The Messiah was on His way! But Jesus didn't stop there; He was not *just* a prophet telling of the future kingdom. He was the Messiah, too! He was and is the King whom they had been anticipating, but He was going to do more than restore the Israelites.

One of Jesus' favorite terms for Himself is "Son of Man." Much debate surrounds what this term means in every case He uses it. Whether His hearers would have always perceived it as a Messianic term is irrelevant here. In certain cases, they certainly would have heard it that way,[54] such as when He says in Mark 13:24-27:

> But in those days, after that tribulation, the sun will be darkened, and the moon will not give its light, and the stars will be falling from heaven, and the powers in the heavens will be shaken. And then they will see the Son of Man coming in clouds with great power and glory. And then He will send out the angels and gather His elect from the four winds, from the ends of the earth to the ends of heaven.

A Jewish hearer would no doubt equate that with the prediction of the coming King in Daniel 7:13-14:

> "I saw in the night visions,
> > and behold, with the clouds of heaven
> there came one like a son of man,
> > and He came to the Ancient of Days
> and was presented before Him.
> > And to Him was given dominion
> and glory and a kingdom,
> > that all peoples, nations, and languages
> should serve Him;
> > His dominion is an everlasting dominion,
> which shall not pass away,
> > and His kingdom one
> that shall not be destroyed.

Here and in many other passages, Jesus is saying that *He* is the One who is going to usher in the Kingdom of God—and in a manner that most had not expected:

> And they were on the road, going up to Jerusalem, and Jesus was walking ahead of them. And they were amazed, and those who followed were afraid. And taking the twelve again, He

began to tell them what was to happen to Him, saying, "See, we are going up to Jerusalem, and the Son of Man will be delivered over to the chief priests and the scribes, and they will condemn Him to death and deliver Him over to the Gentiles. And they will mock Him and spit on Him, and flog Him and kill Him. And after three days He will rise."[55]

The fulfillment of the promise that God made in Genesis 3:15 would happen through the death and resurrection of His Son. That had been the plan all along. That is how God kept His promise to Abraham that all people would be blessed through His bloodline. That is how God established His King; in doing so, His Kingdom was not only for the restoration of the Israelites but also for the restoration of all people who repent and believe the Gospel of Jesus Christ!

After His life-redeeming resurrection, Jesus ascended to the right hand of the Father (Acts 2:33), where He currently rules all of creation as King. He will return, and the Kingdom of God will break into our world once and for all (Isaiah 65:17-25; Revelation 21:1-4). A new creation will be born, and Jesus will destroy sin, death, and Satan. Those who have had faith in Jesus will be in the presence of God forever (Matthew 8:31-38). Until that time, we wait for Jesus to come back. The Holy Spirit guides us to live in the manner worthy of those who know God, in anticipation of the time when sin no longer will inhibit us from doing so (Titus).

King Jesus

The purpose of surveying Biblical history is to establish that Jesus is the King of the Kingdom. It is not myth, metaphor, or allegory; it is the reality that God has given us. It is all over Scripture and in our creeds. The fact that Jesus is King is something that should not be taken lightly and yet is all too often overlooked. We like how Jesus serves us on the cross and makes us right before the Father. Our sinful nature, however, readily denies that Jesus is King of our lives. The Rise of the Individual fuels our denial. Jesus is the Servant-King, but because of sin and the Rise of the Individual, He is Servant alone for far too many of us.

The fact that many people today believe Jesus is their personal Savior is great. He has redeemed them from their sin by His death on the cross: Christianity 101. To have one's relationship with Christ stop there is to see Jesus as Servant alone. He fulfills our need to be right before the Father, which we cannot fulfill by our own devices; however, Jesus is more than that. While personal justification is incredibly important, faith in Christ goes beyond the individual.

Recall what it was like in the first and second chapters in Genesis. God defines life for Adam and Eve; who they are in relation to God (Genesis 1:26); who they are in relation to creation (1:26); their personal identities (1:27, 2:25); their vocations (1:28); what they are to eat (1:29); and their relationship to each other (2:18, 24). In other words, when Adam and Eve were in a perfect personal relationship with God (community), He defined all aspects of life.

When God redeems Israel from slavery in Egypt, He restores their personal relationships with Him. He says that He will be their God, and they will be His people. At that point He again gives them instructions on how to live. God restores the personal relationship, thereby creating community and defining their identities. He also defines how His people live in relation to each other and creation.

At the perfect time, Jesus comes along. Jesus' work of salvation is what makes us acceptable to God. It removes the stench of sin from us in His presence. It restores our personal relationship with God. We need to see Him as God and King here, as Jesus now defines all aspects of life for us in the same manner that Yahweh did in the time before Christ Incarnate. As King, Jesus creates community and defines our identities. He also defines how we are to live in relation to each other and creation.

The idea of Jesus being King may cause some folks to pause because all they can think of is earthly rulers: dictators, monarchies, and governments. After all, isn't that how the Jews of Jesus' time got it wrong? They were expecting the Messiah to be an earthly king, right? That is not the type of

King of which I am speaking. The Kingship of Jesus is much more than that. His seat of power is not one of dominance or control; rather, it is one of love and mercy. God gives us the terms King and Kingdom so that we can better understand His plan in ways familiar to us. Our earthly views of these terms should not corrupt God's truth. Allow me to explain how Jesus functions as King.

The Father rules over His creation and has established the criteria required to be in His Kingdom. We must have His Son, who sits at His right hand as King, advocate for us. The Good News—and I mean Good News—is that *all* who repent and call on the name of Jesus the Christ receive the righteousness that only exists in His victorious death and resurrection (Romans 3:21-26). Jesus is the way to the Father and the Kingdom. He cannot be circumvented, and He is who determines who is in and who is out (Matthew 25:31-46). King Jesus reconciles all those who believe and restores the relationship between Creator and creature.

King Jesus creates the community of the Kingdom, or Kingdom Community. Through His work as Redeemer, we are adopted into the family of God (Galatians 4:1-7)—after having been previously alienated because of sin. We are adopted at the time of baptism, when we are given the benefit of what Jesus has done for us, as if we actually died on the cross ourselves (Romans 6:3-4). Through our baptism and faith, we are brought into the Kingdom Community (1 Corinthians 12:12-13). Lutheran theology holds that baptism is not a decision or an act of the individual but the work of God claiming us as His own and bringing us into His family. It is a promise that God has made to us, that through baptism we are connected to His Son. Baptism therefore becomes the bedrock of faith and the beginning of new life in Christ. It connects followers of Christ to the community He has created. It is the source of our identity in the Kingdom Community.

In the Kingdom Community our identities are wrapped up in Jesus. We already have established that we are in the Kingdom because Jesus forgives our sins and makes us right before the Father. Our baptism makes us adopted sons and daughters. In the Kingdom Community we are, first and foremost, God's family. Jesus brought us into the Kingdom to become sons and daughters, and that is why we are now heirs of the Kingdom alongside Christ (Romans 8:16-17)—the sweetest deal of all time! Living out the will of Christ—being the incarnation of Christ's will—becomes our identity. St. Paul puts it this way: "I have been crucified with Christ. It is no longer I who live, but Christ who lives in me. And the life I now live in the flesh I live by faith in the Son of God, who loved me and gave Himself for me."[56] When King Jesus defines who we are, He also defines our relationship to others and creation.

The thought of being the incarnation of Christ's will raise the question of how exactly that plays out. To examine this question, we may want to look at all of the commands and principles that Jesus has given us; however, we then quickly find ourselves stuck in the mire of trying to figure out what is a command, versus what is a principle. It seems more beneficial at this point then simply to understand that Jesus has given us a filter for the world.

The exact way we see this filter playing out in the world will vary in relation to the traditions that have informed our beliefs and faith practice.[57] Most of the Church, however, should be able to agree on what Scripture says the filter is. Jesus describes it rather directly in Matthew 22:34-40:

> But when the Pharisees heard that He had silenced the Sadducees, they gathered together. And one of them, a lawyer, asked Him a question to test Him. "Teacher, which is the great commandment in the Law?" And He said to Him, "You shall love the Lord your God with all your heart and with all your soul and with all your mind. This is the great and first commandment. And a second is like it: You shall love your neighbor as yourself. On these two commandments depend all the Law and the Prophets."

The expert in the law asks Jesus a question to test Him: what is the most important rule we must follow? What's the deal breaker with God? In response, Jesus quotes the Shema:[58] "Hear, O Israel: The LORD our

God, the LORD is one. You shall love the LORD your God with all your heart and with all your soul and with all your might."[59] It is the anthematic response to the Ten Commandants that Moses delivered to the Israelites in the previous chapter of Deuteronomy. Jesus then follows that command with another that "is like it." From Leviticus 19:18: "You shall not take vengeance or bear a grudge against the sons of your own people, but you shall love your neighbor as yourself: I am the LORD." The phrase "the second is like it" implies equality. The two therefore help define each other. The first command can be better understood in the context of the second, "love your neighbor as yourself," which is better understood in light of the first. Jesus says these are the commands, but they also are the general principles behind the rest of the Law and the Prophets. This is the filter.

Once Jesus gives us this filter, we see how His two commandments sum up all the Law and the Prophets—and probably most directly the Ten Commandments. I believe this can give insight into how Jesus defines the groove for us. In Deuteronomy 5:6 God first establishes that He has redeemed His people and brought them into relationship with Him, thereby creating His community: "'I am the LORD your God, who brought you out of the land of Egypt, out of the house of slavery." He then defines how the individual is to relate to everything around him. The filter of Jesus does the same.

You shall love the Lord your God with all your heart and with all your soul and with all your mind.

> You shall have no other gods before me.

> You shall not take the name of the LORD your God in vain, for the LORD will not hold him guiltless who takes His name in vain.

> You shall not make for yourself a carved image, or any likeness of anything that is in heaven above, or that is on the earth beneath, or that is in the water under the earth. You shall not bow down to them or serve them; for I the LORD your God

am a jealous God, visiting the iniquity of the fathers on the children to the third and fourth generation of those who hate me, but showing steadfast love to thousands of those who love me and keep my commandments.

Observe the Sabbath day, to keep it holy, as the LORD your God commanded you. (The Sabbath theme runs throughout the commands given the Israelites. The Sabbath informed them how to treat themselves, slaves, the poor, the indebted, the foreigner, and the land.)

You shall love your neighbor as yourself.

Honor your father and your mother, as the LORD your God commanded you, that your days may be long, and that it may go well with you in the land that the LORD your God is giving you.

You shall not murder.

And you shall not commit adultery.

And you shall not steal.

And you shall not bear false witness against your neighbor.

And you shall not covet your neighbor's wife. And you shall not desire your neighbor's house, his field, his male servant, his female servant, his ox, his donkey, or anything that is your neighbor's.

In Jesus, God restores the relationship with the individual and creates community. The community is defined by people who are called by God and who put God first and foremost in their lives. Peter expands on the notion of community in his first epistle: "But you are a chosen race, a royal priesthood, a holy nation, a people for His own possession, that you may proclaim the excellencies of Him who called you out of darkness into His marvelous light. Once you were not a people, but now you are God's people; once you had not received mercy, but now you have received mercy."[60]

Community is not simply emotional or cognitive; it is evidenced by worship and respect of the One God and in individuals' love for each other. To clarify: the 'self' with which we love others is not the sinful self, but the God-redeemed self that is part of God's family. We are not to project our sinful desires or inclinations onto others just because we find such sin in ourselves. Instead, we love others within our restored relationship to the Father and reflect His love to them.

As I look groggily in the mirror each morning and see a 35-year-old man with tired eyes and bedhead, I get a reflection of what I am. The reflection is like me, but it isn't actually me. If the reflection I saw in the morning was of a well-groomed man in a tuxedo, the reflection would not be accurate. At the same time, if my wife stood in front of the mirror and saw my 35-year-old face with tired eyes and bedhead, the reflection would not be accurate. The two commands that Jesus gives us as a filter reflect each other in the same manner as me in the morning and my 35-year-old self with tired eyes and bedhead reflection: the commands are like each other, yet they are not one. The commands are the *only* accurate reflections of each other. Something is off if a Christian's love of God is not reflected in his of love of others, or if a Christian's love of others is not reflected in his love of God.

In order then to be in the groove of the Kingdom, we must love God with our whole being and put Him first in our lives. This is evidenced by loving our neighbors as ourselves. We cannot love God and not love others. In reflection, we cannot love others as God loves us without loving God. We need both to live in the groove as King Jesus defines it. The filter that Jesus gives us for the world is the basis for the groove. The groove clearly is not about the individual but about how the individual fits into God's creation. Once that is understood, the applications to vocations and responsibilities are easier to see. This paradigm is freeing but also can be difficult to put into practice.

Distilling all of this down to the basics would be to say that Jesus is my personal Savior and that He is able to be my Savior because He is God and, as such, my Creator. Just like Adam and Eve in the Garden of Eden, I am His creature. Creator and creature together again, without sin getting in the way, is the relationship to which we hope to be restored. That is the goal (Philippians 3:12-21). The problem is: sin *is* in the way, and we are powerless to stop it. We need God to reconcile us to Himself. Jesus is my great Reconciler, and, being reconciled, I have been given new life. Jesus, through the Holy Spirit, has made me a new creature and sustains my new life in Him (2 Corinthians 5:16-17). Jesus, out of His divine love and mercy, has brought us back into the Presence of the Creator, as in the beginning—a virtual return to the Garden. Although this has not yet been fully realized,[61] we have God's promise that it as good as done now.

Once Jesus, our King, places us in the restored Kingdom Community through our baptism, He defines for us what it means to live life as people of the Kingdom. To live in the groove is to be the incarnation of His will. His will is that we love God with all our being and love others as God loves us. His will is evident in the life He lives, and, as His followers and people in His Kingdom, we are expected to live such a life. That is not to say—and some push this idea—that we are Jesus and can do all that He does. What we are to be, though, is the incarnation of His will, doing our best to live in the groove in this sinful world. We are not the Divine Son of God and Son of Man, and we should not expect to be able to do what He is able to do. To think we are able to do that would be to put ourselves in His place, and that is the kind of attitude that got us into this mess in the Garden of Eden.

Jesus being King has implications for His followers. The first is that, when one recognizes Jesus as her Savior, she must also recognize Him as her King; therefore, when she is brought into relationship with Jesus through the Gospel and baptism, she must recognize that she is now part of the King's Kingdom and the community He creates. This seems simple enough; however, many people say they are Christian but reject the Kingdom Community. That signals a serious disconnect. To deny the community is to deny the Kingdom, and to deny the Kingdom puts into question one's relationship with the King.

The Rise of the Individual has made rejection of the Kingdom Community fashionable in our culture, and that rejection takes many forms. The most obvious forms arise in people whose suspicion of authority is so strong that they deny the Kingdom Community simply on face value as *organized religion*. "Organized religion" in this sense becomes a code phrase for an authoritative outside entity. People who follow this line of thinking represent a wide spectrum of belief, from agnostics all the way to those claiming a personal relationship with Jesus. These people often hold faith to be highly personal and individualized; thus, they see the Kingdom Community as a threat to their individuality or "personal faith."

The less obvious forms actually appear inside the Kingdom Community: some Christian leaders reject the Kingdom Community when reacting against tradition or when other leaders appear to hold the Kingdom Community in higher regard than the King. Some Christian communities fall into this trap when they put themselves ahead of the King. Doing so is dangerously shortsighted and denies the Community that the King designed.

Another common, but less extreme, rejection of the Kingdom Community is among people who find faith to be extremely personal and individualized but do not necessarily see the Kingdom Community as a threat to that individuality. They participate in the Kingdom Community on their own terms, often with low levels of commitment or investment, and generally do not view it as an Island in the Confluence. In order to understand how to treat the Kingdom Community as an Island, we need to explore *the* Island in the Confluence.

The Island in the Confluence

The Kingdom Community clearly requires a different type of participation from the individual than the rest of the Confluence— because it is an island. As noted in the description of the Confluence of

Communities, not everyone is treading water. Some individuals are standing on or grasping hold of dry ground. An island exists for the individual because he allows a certain community to influence him openly in defining how he interacts with other communities in the Confluence. He readily accepts this influence. We can see how this is a departure from his normal participation in the Confluence. The Kingdom Community actually is not *an* island; it is *the* Island. Other islands exist in the Confluence, as well. Such islands are in competition with the Kingdom Community. We now will look at what it means to be on the Island of the Kingdom Community in the Confluence, as well as how other islands function.

When the Holy Spirit sweeps an individual out of the Confluence onto the Island of the Kingdom Community, his role in the community is different than when he is freely wading in the Confluence. Before, he was able to customize his communities as he saw fit in pursuit of the Divine Dream. Now, his identity is created and determined by an outside force, something bigger and external to himself, namely King Jesus. On the Island of the Kingdom Community, Jesus defines who the individual is and what his role is to be, both in the Kingdom Community and in the rest of the Fluid Confluence.[62] In other words, when he receives the forgiveness of Jesus, he also agrees to allegiance to and identification with the Community, as Jesus defines that Community; moreover, the Kingdom Community becomes the primary community in his life.

"Primary community" means that all involvement with other communities in the Confluence becomes secondary. Secondary communities are subject to the ideas, core values, and assumptions of the Kingdom Community. The Kingdom Community, because it is an island, now openly influences the individual, and the individual readily accepts such influence. It is solid ground on which she can stand in the Confluence. She normally would customize her communities as she saw fit; however, on the Island, assimilation and subjugation to the attractive aspects of her chosen communities is only possible when those aspects do not compete with aspects of the Kingdom Community. Let's take a look at Nancy's life to see how this works.

After lots of deliberation, Nancy decides to go to the protest outside Meyers Packing. She does not participate, but she decides to be more open to the ideas of her friends. After all, she has known some of them for a long time, and they are some of the people she is closest to. She starts doing some online research about animal cruelty in the farming industry, and the positions of her friends start to make more sense to her. Soon, she is a full-fledged vegan.

Her decisions to become vegan and to protest animal cruelty in the food industry lead to more awkward situations with her father. She and her dad finally have a heated argument. A lot of things come out that both of them have long suppressed. For the first time in a long time, really since the death of her mother, she and her dad actually communicate. After hashing things out, their relationship starts to heal, and a few months later Nancy is even back in church. She feels that she cannot go back to the Catholic Church, but she realizes she has been blaming God for a lot of things in life instead of turning to Him in tough times. She grows rapidly in her faith, with the solid teaching and personal support she finds in her new church community.

She occasionally wonders whether she even should be vegan anymore. She doesn't know any other practicing Christians who are vegan. She has some good talks with her pastor about it, and her friends in her Church community affirm her choice; nothing in Scripture prohibits being vegan. She therefore is at peace with it, until Todd, one of her vegan kayaking friends, comes up with a plan to get rid of Meyers Packing once and for all.

Todd says it will be easy. All they need to do is wait until the night security guard takes his break, then sneak in and start the fire. Being a firefighter, Todd knows how to do it and get away with it. No one will get hurt, but the financial loss will kill the company. Nancy isn't the only one to tell Todd that she isn't comfortable with the plan; others keep talking about the risks involved. All Nancy can think about is how this is not right. She doesn't want Meyers Packing around, but there is no way she can get behind this. Breaking in and destroying property? Out of the question! That isn't what Jesus would want her to do. Now the question is: what will she do if her friends go through with the plan?

The King brings Nancy back to the solid ground of the Island of the Kingdom Community. When she is on the Island, the Kingdom Community becomes her primary community, but she can still stick a foot or both hands or her head or most of herself in the Confluence. She must stay connected to the Island, though, since that is the source of what shapes and influences her. In doing so, she willingly begins to assimilate to the groove of life as King Jesus defines it. Some of the values that she has assumed are that she should not break governmental law and should not destroy her neighbor's property.

For our purposes, we can picture Nancy with one foot on the Island and one in the Confluence. While she has willingly become subject to the assumptions, ideas, and core values of the Island, she also has been customizing the secondary communities in which she takes part. She has stuck one toe in veganism and has assumed that community's value of opposing animal cruelty. She would like to shut down Meyers Packing, and this is where her being on the Island becomes evident. She might have decided previously to go along with Todd's plan or to weigh participation against obvious risks; however, now she would not go along with it because it goes against the values of the Island. To be on the Island is to allow the King to define her values.

The Kingdom Community therefore creates a tension for all individuals, especially enhanced in the Modern West. Jesus calls us to be His sheep, while Nietzsche told us that sheep are sick herd animals. We hear Jesus, but Nietzsche is whispering in our subconscious. While most people recognize Western individualism, most of us do not know just how much it influences us every day. The Fluid Confluence reinforces the Americanized worldview that identity for the individual is internal and trumps allegiance with any one group. In that context, the idea of the Kingdom Community being an Island with a King comes across as totalitarian, controlling, and legalistic, not only to those without faith in Christ but also to those with faith. In short, we avoid a God who expects us to give up the Divine Dream in order to be with Him. We prefer a convenient God who fits into *our* Divine Dream and plays the roles we give Him.

When that battle rages in our heads and hearts, we often look for excuses to ignore the Kingdom Community. The excuse that probably tops the list for most is that being part of the Community is not necessary as long as we have Jesus. This leads to an interesting distinction that my Lutheran sensibilities must make. Participation in the Kingdom Community is not a thing we do that keeps us in a relationship with Jesus, although it certainly helps grow a healthy relationship. The Lutheran view of righteousness says that Jesus is the only way to be right with the Father and that nothing we do can add to our righteousness or gain us forgiveness. The abuse of that true gospel, however, has led to the phenomenon of "cheap grace," wherein head-knowledge faith is considered essential, while personal formation within the Community—including accountability for sin—is not necessary and could even be detrimental to faith. While I believe the Lutheran view of righteousness to be correct, stopping there means ignoring much of what Scripture says about the relationships among God, creature, and creation.[63] The Island of the Kingdom Community is not a requirement but a gift from the King, the value of which is obvious, compared with other islands in the Confluence.

Jesus places us on the Island. We do not learn His ways, live them, and thereby *earn* or *achieve* a place on the Island. On the contrary, Christ is the one who restores the relationship between Creator and creature, placing us by His grace alone on the Island first. We then are allowed the fantastic opportunity of having the King teach us how the world works and how we are to live in it. Therein lies the main difference between the Island of the Kingdom Community and all other islands: the criteria for getting on and staying on the Island hinge on Jesus' role in the individual's life.

Jesus both initiates and maintains the relationship. The only way off the Island is for an individual to jump back into the Confluence and deny his relationship with King Jesus.

Being on every other island in the Confluence depends on the individual's participation in a community. An island like this exists for the individual because he allows a community to form his identity and define how he interacts with other communities in the Confluence. Some communities, such as religions and philosophies (Islam, Buddhism, and so forth), exist solely to be islands. Other islands are more like shallow sandbars. They are normally regular streams, or communities, but are turned into islands by individuals who stand on the submerged sandbar. This type of island is often harder to identify because of its easily concealed nature.

For island-only communities, such as Islam or Buddhism, the individual enters an island by doing and fulfilling the requirements of that island and allowing the community to define his interactions with the rest of the Confluence. As long as he is doing what that island asks, and that community defines his interactions in the Confluence, he remains on that island and is part of that community; however, if he stops practicing and no longer lets that community define him, he is off the island *and* out of the community. These islands are easy to see and may seem like sure footing. They all rely on the individual, though, so they lack the rock-solid assurance that King Jesus and His Island offer.

In the case of a regular stream-turned-island, the individual can change his participation, have the stream no longer be an island for him, and still take part in the community. When he steps off the submerged sandbar, that stream simply becomes another customizable community in the Confluence for him. Here is an example from Wisconsin of a regular stream-turned-island for Jake.

> Jake was eleven years old when the Green Bay Packers won the Super Bowl with Brett Favre in 1997. He has been a diehard fan ever since. It surprises some people at the bar when he chimes in during an argument about the secondary or fourth-quarter

calls because he doesn't seem like a typical Packers fan—or even a sports fan, for that matter. He can hold his own, though, and can list players and stats that many fans have to look up.

He probably is able to do so because he has had a pretty strict football regimen for the past three years. It goes year-round but really picks up midsummer when he starts working on his fantasy football picks. He creates a list of Packers, ranking them by position and availability. In order to do that and to know who's who, he watches coverage on sports channels every night and listens to sports talk radio every morning. Jake then watches every game, including the preseason.

Loraine isn't much of a football fan, but she has learned just by being around Jake that talking is not allowed during SportsCenter; that the Bears, Vikings, and Lions (in that order) are the enemy; and that, even though Brett Favre once was beloved, he is now the devil and probably a terrorist.

While Jake may not look like a Packers fan in the bar most days, game days are a different story. *Everything* is scheduled around the Packers game: no pool playing, no shopping, no homework, no night classes, no band practice, no family events, no leaving the apartment. He has cable television just so that he can watch every game through different cable options. During the game, Jake parks himself in his recliner wearing an Aaron Rodgers jersey and his lucky Packers hat. If people want to fill in the space around him, that's fine, as long they aren't Bears, Vikings, or Lions fans and are quiet during the game and instant replays. Jake is usually pretty subdued and mild mannered, but when the Packers are playing he yells at the television like he is getting paid to coach the team.

Jake's participation in the community of Green Bay Packers fans is an island for him. He willingly submits to the community's core values, assumptions, and ideas, and he knowingly allows the Packers to define his interaction with the other communities he encounters in the Confluence. If he no longer allowed the Packers to influence his other interactions, he would no longer be on that island; the Packers would just become another one of his customized communities; the island would return to being a stream in the Confluence. While the Packers are his island, his involvement in the community is a form of idolatry, as is being on any island other than the Kingdom Community. Shallow sandbars are never meant to be islands. Like every other island that is not the Kingdom Community, these streams-turned-islands are not actually solid ground, and considering them as such is the equivalent of chasing false gods. The only island we are to have is the one created, defined, and sustained by Jesus the King. The Island of the Kingdom Community is the only truly solid ground in the Confluence.

Notice also the differences between Jake's and Nancy's examples. Having the Packers as an island, Jake sees his participation in the Confluence in black-and-white terms. Any community that creates a conflict for him being on the island of the Packers loses out. If it did not, he no longer would be on the Packer island. Nancy, however, struggles with the tensions between the Kingdom Community and the other communities in her life.

In fact, the groove of the Kingdom Community actually requires that she dip into the Confluence and live out the groove in her other communities. Like Jake, she attempts to give precedence to the groove of the Island in all her communities as she evaluates what routes the King would have her take. Unlike Jake's island, though, the Kingdom Community recognizes that Nancy is going to fail to put the groove first in all her communities. This highlights one of the beauties of the Kingdom Community that makes it distinctive: even though Nancy will make mistakes in her choices, these mistakes do not disqualify her from being on the Island. When she confesses and repents of her sin she is given reassurance in her relationship with the King. At the same time, through the process of repentance, her relationship with others on the Island is strengthened. We have begun to explore what life on the Island is like, so let us give it more in-depth attention.

Part Five:
Life on the Island of the Kingdom Community

Who?

So far, we have observed the Rise of Individual, the Transition from Modern Thought, the Fluid Confluence of Communities, the Rise of the King, and the Island of the Kingdom Community. You may be either bored out of your gourd or saying to yourself, "That's interesting, but what's the point?" You also may want to understand the Island of the Kingdom Community in more concrete terms. We will address these questions as we see how our observations apply to our own lives, and we also will see what all of this means for the Church. First, we will grapple with "who" the Kingdom Community is. To do so, let's take a peek into Nancy's life on the Island.

> Nancy felt like her mind was wandering a bit as she sat during an extended prayer time in worship, but she remembered what her pastor told her about prayer: "If you're thinking about something, you probably need to talk it over with God. Try to pray it out." She remembers a lot of the things her pastor says; he has always been helpful and caring. *Thank you, Lord, for Pastor Paul.*
>
> She can't really recall anything the priests said in Catholic Mass when she was growing up, just a lot of stuff about Mary and St. Some-Such—then again, she wasn't paying attention,

either. *Father, I am sorry that I didn't pay attention the first time you were trying to reach me.* She did remember the confessional though. Most kids hated it, but she had always kind of looked forward to it. She always felt somehow cleaner after confessing and hearing absolution. She also finds the words of the corporate confession to be very powerful: "I confess to almighty God and to you, my brothers and sisters, that I have greatly sinned." She wishes Bethlehem Church practiced confession and absolution—without all the "Hail Mary" stuff, of course—but she doesn't think Baptists really do that. As it is, she feels like people stare at her when she crosses herself; however, she feels like it marks her as one participating in the blessing and isn't going to give it up. Maybe she will talk to Pastor Paul about it.

For the most part, she loves Bethlehem. She is happy to have found a church home after looking at several. She loves the energy and the music, the emphasis on Bible study, and the hunger to seek and share the gospel with the lost. She was lost herself not so long ago. *Lord Jesus, thank you so much for saving me from myself and bringing me to Bethlehem Church. Thank you for Bethlehem. Show me how I can serve you better every day.*

Her father has come to worship with her several times. She was hoping that he might "see the light" and leave the Catholic Church for Bethlehem. He said the people were very nice, but he missed the Catholic liturgy. In the end he said it was just too weird for him and that she should come back to St. Dominic. They had some long talks about it, and, although she doesn't understand why he won't change, she knows that Jesus loves him and that he loves Jesus. *God, thank you for my dad; watch over and protect him.*

She even found a friend here—Sue, who kayaks! *Lord, thank you for Sue, and thank you for kayaking. Please let me race my best next weekend.* She has to remember to get everything ready, as this is the first time she and Sue are going to race a relay together. That's right! She needs to go to the store, pack, make sure she has direction . . . . *Father, help me to keep all the things in my life in the proper perspective.* She wonders if Todd is going to be there. She hasn't talked to him since she refused to go in on the plan to burn down Meyers Packing. Todd didn't go through with it, but she isn't sure why. *Jesus, give me the courage and the words to talk to Todd.*

By now, many readers will have made the connection that the Kingdom Community is the catholic[64] and apostolic Church. From here on, I will use the terms Church and Kingdom Community interchangeably. I have avoided using the term "church" thus far to describe the Community because the term has associated baggage for a lot of people today. Church has become something that we define, and, while defining it has its benefits, our definitions often omit the Kingship of Jesus. As King, Jesus creates the Community, defines our identities, and defines how we are to live in relation to each other and creation. In other words, He defines the Church. The simple answer, therefore, as to "who" composes the Kingdom Community, is people like Nancy, reconciled to the Father by the death and resurrection of His Son Jesus, adopted into the Kingdom by baptism, and living as new creatures in Christ. Knowing that, we still need clarity on how Methodists, Baptists, Lutherans, Catholics, Pentecostals, and everyone in between coexist on the Island.

Ecumenism, the effort to unite all Christian denominations, has been much debated in the past sixty years. I am not arguing for or against ecumenism, which has emphatic proponents and opponents; I am just laying out how the Island of the Kingdom Community works in the Confluence. If the Kingdom Community comprises people like Nancy—and is not a physical building or an authoritative institution—then we need something that enables us to identify who exactly is on the Island. Once we establish that, the role of denominational institutions, or streams of Christianity,[65] in the Confluence becomes clear.

We cannot know what is in an individual's heart, so faith in King Jesus is invisible to observers. God knows whether someone is on the Island; we do not. A visible marker of her faith therefore becomes necessary. I suggest a marker such as the Nicene Creed, a simple confession of faith covering the basics of how God created the world to work.

> We believe in one God,
> the Father, the Almighty,
> maker of heaven and earth,
> of all that is, seen and unseen.
>
> We believe in one Lord, Jesus Christ,
> the only Son of God,
> eternally begotten of the Father,
> God from God, light from light,
> true God from true God,
> begotten, not made,
> being of one substance with the Father;
> by Him all things were made.
> For us and for our salvation
> He came down from heaven,
> was incarnate by the Holy Spirit and the virgin Mary
> and became truly human.
> For our sake He was crucified under Pontius Pilate;
> He suffered death and was buried.
> On the third day He rose again
> in accordance with the Scriptures;
> He ascended into heaven
> and is seated at the right hand of the Father.
> He will come again in glory to judge the living and the dead,
> and His kingdom will have no end.
>
> We believe in the Holy Spirit, the Lord and giver of life,
> who proceeds from the Father [and the Son],[66]
> who with the Father and the Son is worshiped and glorified,
> who has spoken through the prophets.

We believe in one holy catholic[67] and apostolic Church.
We acknowledge one baptism for the forgiveness of sins.
We look for the resurrection of the dead,
and the life of the world to come. Amen.

Using this simple confession as historically understood by the Church, denominational barriers to the Island are removed.[68] It gives all those whom Christ has swept onto the Island a common tie. Pretending that differences do not still exist, however, is foolish. In order to move past the differences, we need to reframe how we see them. Most Christians view their particular stream of Christianity as an island, and that is where the confusion begins.

We should instead see each stream of Christianity as a secondary community in the Fluid Confluence—that is, the most important secondary community, but still only a secondary community. As stated earlier, making any community other than the Kingdom Community into an island is idolatry, and the same rule applies here. Subordinating denominational communities does not diminish their roles but ultimately puts King Jesus at the head of each and every Christian community, thereby having a twofold effect on how we view the Church.

First, placing Jesus before the various streams of Christianity allows us to see that no particular version of Christianity has a monopoly on the King. One can strengthen one's relationship with Jesus in any Christian community that is in submission to the Kingdom Community. We see this in Nancy's example. She may not understand why her father chose to remain Catholic rather than becoming Baptist like she did, but she recognizes the fact that he has a relationship with Christ through the Catholic Church.

Second, ranking the streams of Christianity below the larger Kingdom Community more accurately reflects the lives and attitudes of believers, most of whom find aspects of multiple Christian communities comfortable. Believers' ability to be at home in multiple streams of Christianity is the result of individuals customizing various communities, as well as the fact that these communities actually do share the same Holy Spirit. The individual cannot customize the Kingdom Community—to do so would be to rise against the King—but she can customize her secondary communities in accordance to the groove of the Island. Nancy's prayer time illustrates this: she has no problem with crossing herself or desiring confession and absolution in her Baptist community, even though such ideas differ from, and may even go against, some of the practices in that Christian community.

Since the Kingdom Community is not an institution but rather a body of people, being on the Island is about being with people, not belonging to an organization. On the Island we are inseparably linked to each other (1 Corinthians 12). The desire of the individual is placed last after God and others. It is a total reversal from the normal role the individual plays in the Fluid Confluence, where the individual pursues his own Divine Dream. The idea of the individual believer is foreign in Old Testament period Judaism and in the early Church. On the Island we are constantly being shaped and refined into what someday we will be when King Jesus returns—people without sin living together in the Kingdom with the Triune God for eternity. Our participation in the Confluence should reflect that reality.

Christians therefore need to be in community with other Christians in order to exercise their beliefs. In fact, Christian communities play an incredibly important role in the Confluence. These communities are where the ideas, assumptions, and core values of the Kingdom Community are first lived out while this world remains. They give us an initial framework of what being on the Island means, as well as the opportunity to employ the gifts of the Island, such as forgiveness, worship, mercy, love, and discipleship.

Playing upon John Locke's logic, however, we realize that all communities are *not* created equal. Size and age are not necessarily determining factors. A group of twenty Christians with no formal name may be healthier and closer to the groove of the Island than a twenty thousand-person megachurch—or *vice versa*. The interplay of differing Christian communities, as well as their strengths and weaknesses in the

Confluence, is a subject that demands more attention than we can give here. How each model works as a secondary community and how they work together is complex. For now, we are at least able to see a bit more concretely "who" the Kingdom Community is.

Now that we have an idea of "who" the Island is, the time is right to ask some introspective questions before we move on to what existing in the larger Confluence means for the Island of the Kingdom Community. Consider:

> How do you view yourself? Are you the star of your own movie?
>
> How does God view you and what role has He given you?
>
> If one of the communities in your life asked you to move away to another location for five years, would you go?
>
> What if a Christian community of a different stream than your own asked you for a commitment of your time, treasure, or talent? Would you give it?
>
> Is Jesus both King and Servant in your life, or just Servant?

These questions are supposed to be difficult. I think all of us know what the answers are *supposed* to be but are unable to answer honestly. We constantly struggle with keeping our priorities straight and not falling into idolatry. The problem is that the Fluid Confluence makes idolatry so easy. Either we make ourselves into gods as we move about the Confluence pursuing our Divine Dreams, or we turn communities into islands and make them our gods. Doing so directly conflicts with the teachings of King Jesus. There is only one Triune God. Jesus created one Island Community, into which each Christian has been placed, and He defines our roles in the Confluence.

Life on the Island does not fit the norms of the rest of the Confluence, that is, the world in which we in the West live. Do we therefore cloister ourselves and wait for Christ to return? Certainly not! We have observed how we arrived at this state, as well as how individuals navigate the Confluence, so now we can step back and discern our own way in the Confluence, according to the groove of the Island. The way we are to live out the groove in the Confluence is a Life of Worship.

Free to Serve: A Life of Worship

"You shall love the Lord your God with all your heart and with all your soul and with all your mind. This is the great and first commandment." Jesus is describing a Life of Worship—24/7—not sitting in a pew singing hymns day and night, but a life wholly devoted to glorifying God and His will. Such a life flies in the face of the compartmentalization that the Confluence fosters, but we are called to live out the groove in the Confluence. Our entire lives are Worship. Let's take a little lengthier look at Nancy's life to see how the Life of Worship begins to play out.

After worship at Bethlehem, Nancy talks with Sue about their upcoming race and finalizes their plans. They figure out who is bringing what and when they are going to leave. The week passes quickly, and, before she knows it, the eve of the trip has arrived. As she packs, she thinks to herself that, previously, during the week of a race, work always dragged, but now it seems to fly by. She thinks that only one explanation is possible—purpose.

A year ago, some friends from Bethlehem told her that her everyday job was actually God-pleasing work. Can you imagine that! Working in a bank is serving God! It took some prayer, but, after a while, her attitude at work started to change. Sure, she still gets frustrated and bored like everyone else, but the idea that she is serving God just by doing her job gives her a real sense of purpose. She had always been what she considered to be a good employee, but now she feels like she is more. She has taken it on herself to foster a great work environment

70

for everyone and even talks to her "work friends" like actual friends. The sense of purpose has to be why weeks fly by now.

She finishes packing everything for the race, gets ready for bed, and spends some time talking with God. She wakes up the next morning like most, realizing she fell asleep while praying. She supposes there could be worse things. After her morning routine, she looks out the window just as Sue is pulling up. Perfect timing! Then again, she does still have to double-check everything and actually get it outside, so she feels a bit rushed.

Sue and Meghan greet her in her driveway. Nancy had heard a lot about Meghan from Sue but hadn't met her until now. She seems nice enough. They load Nancy's gear and start off on a scenic, two-and-a-half hour drive.

Meghan is more outgoing than Nancy and initiates a lot of conversation. The talk in the car goes all over the place and eventually lands on faith. Sue and Meghan used to belong to the same church years ago, but Meghan got married and started going to her husband's church across town. Meghan was raised Baptist and now attends a Lutheran church; this sparks all sorts of questions from Nancy. The three of them have a great talk about what they believe and what Jesus has done in their lives. The conversation eventually leads to Nancy's uneasiness about the possibility of seeing Todd and the others this weekend. Both Sue and Meghan have some uplifting encouragement for her, and, before she knows it, they are at the river. As they get out, Nancy glances at Meghan, and she smiles back at her. Nancy thinks to herself how weird it is never to have met this woman face to face until three hours ago and now feel so connected to her.

A few of her vegan friends are there, and she soon hears the gossip about Todd and how he had gone a little off the deep end. Turns out he hadn't gone through with the fire at the packing plant because no one would help him. Some people are mad at him for suggesting the plan, and Todd is mad at everybody for not supporting him. Todd surprises everyone and appears for the race, but he is off by himself all day.

Nancy doesn't like the tension in the group and isn't sure what Todd thinks of her right now. She thinks about something Pastor Paul says: "Hard conversations make messes that lead to healing." She doesn't like hard conversations and doesn't want things to get messy; however, her relationship with Todd isn't going to heal itself.

"Todd!" Nancy approaches him from behind, and he spins quickly when she speaks. "I'm sorry that my not helping with the plan hurt you. It wasn't my intention. I value your friendship. Please forgive me."

"Nancy, I appreciate your coming over here, but I am sick and tired of all of you pretending like you want to do something about animal cruelty. I came up with a great plan to do something about it for real, and you guys treated me like a wingnut."

"I can't speak for the others, but I really do want to stop animal cruelty. I don't think you're a wingnut, either. I think you're a man of action. I would like to act, too, but I want to figure out a way to approach this situation with love and understanding for all involved." Nancy isn't sure about saying that last part.

"Love for all involved! Love for all involved! You want to *love* those murderers at Meyers Packing? Not me! They are the enemy!," exclaims Todd, slack-jawed and wide-eyed.

She thinks: okay, here goes. "Yes, I am trying to love them. I am trying to see them the way Jesus sees me and you and love them. That's why I didn't help you; it's not the type of thing Jesus has prepared for me to do. Besides, you sound like you want to hurt them now. You don't actually want to hurt them, do you, Todd?"

Todd had never heard Nancy talk about Jesus before. He and his friends know she is going to church now because she is always talking about doing this or that, but until now she hasn't been so upfront with it. "No, I don't want to hurt anyone. I'm just ticked off. But I don't love them, either."

Nancy senses Todd's avoidance of her mentioning Jesus, so she decides not to push. "How about this then—you and I work together to figure out a way to stop the animal cruelty in a way that we both can get behind?"

Todd mellows considerably. "I suppose that would work. Just know that I am going to hold you to that."

"Deal. And you know that I am not done talking about Jesus with you, right?" Nancy wonders why saying "Jesus" out loud is so hard.

"I figured as much, Nance—I figured," Todd responds, sounding rather nonplussed.

At the campfire that night, Nancy is sitting next to Sue, who is next to Meghan. Todd comes up, sits next to Nancy, and asks her how her race went that day. As they are talking, Sue leans over and whispers into Meghan's ear, "Oh, he's cute!"

This vignette from Nancy's life illustrates that a Life of Worship has different manifestations. The first, corporate worship, is probably the easiest to distinguish. Corporate worship is the time—often formal but not always—when Christians come together to worship God. Worship takes many forms because it is easily customized to each community in the Confluence. Various Christian communities have different opinions on the essential components of worship and the interpretation and style of those components. Most agree that the presence of the Word is necessary, and, after that, the most common elements are music, prayer, and regular celebration of the Lord's Supper.

Other elements of a Life of Worship are harder to distinguish from each other than corporate worship is, although the Modern world has tried to separate them. These elements fall under the rubric of discipleship and, for the most part, fit nicely into the second great commandment of Jesus: "You shall love your neighbor as yourself." In Nancy's example we can pick out tidbits of service, vocation, evangelism, personal devotion, fellowship of believers, and reconciliation. Even after listing those categories, though, strictly defining when she is doing what is difficult. That's okay—in fact, it's great! We will see shortly how defining terms for discussion and clear teaching is an important practice; however, the idea that we can clearly categorize every moment of our lives is simply a fallacy promoted by Modernism. This book makes the plea that a follower of Christ needs to be on the Island, and the best way to begin living out the groove of the Island is to remove compartmentalization from the individual's life.

This freeing, scary, messy concept is one that the Church must recognize and fully embrace. It is not a new idea; however, Modernism has eroded it to the point of being an afterthought on "Stewardship Sunday" sermons in statements like "Remember, everything is God's." Its practice is so foreign in the Confluence that even the Church has a hard time understanding it now. Being Free to Serve is a simple concept that has far-reaching implications and creates a world of mess for most of today's Western Christian communities.

Freedom to Serve begins with personal identity. The individual recognizes that she is first and foremost an adopted child of God. She therefore is going to live her life according to the ways of her family (the Kingdom Community). She views everything—and I mean everything— in her life through that filter. She sees all that she has and does as God-given gifts and responsibilities. As she lives out the groove of the Island, exercising and tending to those God-given gifts and responsibilities, she is serving King Jesus and living Worship. Sometimes that Worship seems obvious: Nancy goes to corporate worship; she spends time in prayer; she shares Jesus with a friend. Most times, though, Worship may not be obvious to our compartmentalizing minds: she worships as she packs her gear, does her morning routine, works at the bank, talks with friends, shares during the car ride, and enjoys creation.

I may seem to be saying that just living is worshiping God. In a sense that is true—taking care of your God-given responsibilities is Worship. This definition of worship, however, does not mean that people off of the Island are able to worship God by just living. People off of the Island are able to fulfill the will of God without knowing Him. This is not Worship, though, because nonbelievers are missing the first great commandment of Jesus' filter. On the other hand, one's life can change. Nancy's life shifts once King Jesus restores her relationship with Him. At that point Nancy is shown the groove of the Island. She comes to know God and becomes aware of her purpose in the Kingdom of God. She is then able to recognize that she can live a Life of Worship by following God's will. Living in the groove becomes a *purposeful* response to being swept up on the Island by Jesus through the Holy Spirit.

On the Island, the Holy Spirit enables Nancy to live a purposeful Life of Worship for the glory of God. She is strengthened in knowing that, by doing so, she is preparing herself and this world for the time when King Jesus breaks in with His Kingdom once and for all. With the relationship restored she can recognize that washing the dishes, cleaning the garage, brushing her teeth, and picking up after the dog are in fact Worship. Working out, racing her kayak, and sitting around the campfire with friends are indeed Worship. They are all examples of the gifts and responsibilities that God has given His children. She can find peace and joy in her responsibilities because tending to them is serving the King and worshiping Him.

Sometimes people who are attempting to live their lives in this manner are called "Super-Christians" by both people within and outside the Church. I find that term to be sad commentary on the state of the Church. Most people today do not see the necessity of making the Kingdom

Community an Island that is the center of the believer's life. Making the Kingdom Community one's Island is considered going above and beyond what is essential. Today's expectation is that believers—nonprofessional church workers—are to keep their faith life relegated to Sundays, churches, holidays, ministries, and so on, not have it pervade all areas of life. Such compartmentalizing prevents people from being Free to Serve. Even— perhaps especially—most professional church workers are not really Free to Serve.

Most Christian communities expect their paid leaders to be "Super-Christians"—not because they live a Life of Worship but because they are to live a life of definable, documentable acts of service. This expectation happens for a host of reasons, from churches succumbing to an element of modern culture to trying to get the most out of their employees. Whatever the reason, it creates an unhealthy imbalance in the lives of Christian leaders. People with tremendous spiritual gifts can become burned out to the point of being numb in ministry. When a worker becomes numb, he begins to validate his vocation by volume of work, and people become tasks instead of people.

Worse yet is that in many Christian communities this kind of "Super-Christian" is the role model and pinnacle for discipleship. The person caught in this life may even be worse off than the nonprofessional church worker in terms of Worship. He may be fooling himself that all his acts of service can *only* be done by him, so that, when he does them, he is fulfilling his God-given purpose. Meanwhile, he may ignore or degrade other God-given gifts and responsibilities, such as family, health, and personal relationships. I think the Church knows this is inherently wrong. Many, if not most, Lutheran (Missouri Synod) conferences that I have attended have focused on time management, the Sabbath, or the physical and mental health of pastoral and professional church workers.

We have allowed the Confluence to inform how the people on the Island should live. People within the Church are so engrossed in the Confluence that the compartmentalization of communities has become the norm in Christian communities. Our attempt to counteract it actually promotes the danger of compartmentalization that we are fighting: often, when Christian communities attempt to bring balance back into their communities, they actually end up working against a Life of Worship by making any cause, hobby, demographic group, or service into a ministry. Nancy discovers this at Bethlehem.

> To stay in shape for kayaking, Nancy started running in the morning. She loves it. She does it five times a week. She feels great afterward. She notices that she has been praying sometimes while she runs. Once in a while, she runs with Todd.
>
> During a sermon about stewardship of time, Nancy starts to wonder if she should be running; after all, it takes up five hours a week. After the service she has a quick talk with Pastor Paul and sets up a meeting later that week.
>
> Nancy arrives at the meeting a little nervous, thinking that Pastor Paul is going to tell her to stop wasting her time running. Running is frivolous, and she could be working in a soup kitchen somewhere instead. She is surprised by Pastor Paul's greeting, though.
>
> "Nancy, I didn't know you were a runner! So am I!
>
> After about 15 minutes of exchanging training details and history, Pastor Paul exclaims, "You know what we should do, Nancy? We should start a running ministry! I know of at least ten other people in the church who would love to join."
>
> Fifteen minutes later, Nancy shuts the door behind her as the head of "Beautiful Feet," the new running ministry at Bethlehem Church.

The Holy Spirit is alive and active in the lives of Christians. As a result, we feel like we are pulled, tugged, and attracted toward different things in life. Some things seem obviously of God and others are less clear, but in all things we should seek to discern the will of God through His Word, prayer, and discussion with our Christian community. As most Christian communities in the Confluence exercise this discernment, they normally bring things into the organization of the Christian community when they are deemed God's will. This is usually how things like prison ministries, homeless-shelter ministries, food-drive ministries, and blind ministries get started. An individual from a Christian community may minister to others in these ways on his own and think of them as being Island-related. Chances are that he will not, though, and will end up only doing such things in the context of a "ministry" in his Christian community.

A Christian community also may deem as the will of God things that are less service-oriented and bring them into the organization of the Christian community. This is how basketball ministries, sewing ministries, men's ministries, family-life ministries, and the like get started. An individual may play basketball with his Christian community and think it is Island-related, then play basketball at the park with some friends and think it has nothing to do with the Island. How confusing! Because he is immersed in the Confluence, he will see no problem with this compartmentalizing. He designates what times and activities of his life are God's, and the others are his to do with as he wills. The effect of compartmentalization on the Church is that it has the opposite outcome of a Life of Worship. The Church should do all it can to address this as the most serious threat and roadblock to discipleship and a Life of Worship.

If the Church is going to fight compartmentalization and really promote a Life of Worship, it is going to have to give up some control. It is going to have to allow a decentralization of some of its current activities. In the future it should avoid pulling so many things into the organization of Christian communities in order to make them feel legitimate for Christians. Instead, Christian communities should focus on a few ministries and do them well. Such ministries are the types that benefit from that specific Christian community coming together and giving the ministry its all. We constantly need to instill in people that King Jesus has redeemed their *whole* life, not just certain elements, places, and times. We need to teach and preach the whole Word of God in ways that equip people to live their lives through the lens of the Kingdom Community. This training cannot be done from the pulpit alone, or only with head knowledge, but must be demonstrated through life-sized modeling. Life-sized modeling is a form of discipleship in which Christians are involved in other Christians'[69] lives so that they are able to show each other how to live out the will of King Jesus in real time.

Leaders of Christian communities may be reading this and thinking, "If my pastor is off tending to his gifts and responsibilities, or 'life-sized modeling,' how will everything be accomplished?" Pastors may be thinking, "This is all well and good, but, if my people are off living a Life of Worship, how will I know they are growing in their faith?" These are fair questions that need to be addressed.

I urge pastors and other paid leaders to sit down and go over whatever agreement or contract they have made or will make. What vocation does the agreement specifically spell out? Are there examples of the duties of that vocation scripturally and in the early Church? What duties does this community expect? How do the expected duties fit into a typical week? How does that work week fit into the Biblical description of a leader having his life and household in order (Life of Worship)?[70] Going through this exercise should bring some clarity as to what a leader is supposed to be doing vocationally. If the duties expected from the community are outside the vocation, then someone else needs to do it or the duties need to be eliminated. The duties probably either belong to another vocation or are a customizable aspect of the community. If the duties fall under the vocation of the leader and he is unable to live a Life of Worship while fulfilling his vocational responsibilities, then at least one more person must come alongside him to help shoulder the load.

I have no delusions about the difficulty of this process. Following these steps in most long-established Christian communities will be hard and messy because people will not want to change. We are not called to a life that is easy and neat, however. We are called to live new lives on the

Island and take direction from our King, Jesus. Until He returns, we need to deal head on with the messes that sin creates.

When this first step begins to be established (it will surely be a lengthy process, like a slow "trust fall"), then one can start to answer the next question: "If my people are off living a Life of Worship, how will I know they are growing in their faith?" To start, decentralizing some activities from the Christian community does not mean disbanding the community altogether. Far from it! Certain elements of the Life of Worship we can only get from Christian communities, like corporate worship and scriptural studies. These activities are incredibly important and actually inform us as to how to live out the groove of the Island, which is a Life of Worship. Many leaders at this point will say, "I'll see my people at worship and Bible study? That changes nothing then," or, "I'll see my people at worship and Bible study? That would be great!" I understand those sentiments, but remember that pastors have added the Life of Worship to their preaching and teaching. While they are encouraging their people to live a Life of Worship, they also are doing so. That means that, instead of trying to bring people (from within and without) to their Christian community for everything, pastors ideally are living a Life of Worship among them.

It sounds simple, but this paradigm has tremendous implications. Pastors are in the Confluence with their parishioners, as well as with nonbelievers, and can take the groove of the Island from their Christian communities' buildings right into the communities in others' lives. It reinforces and instills the way of the Island, often with no formal teaching time. At the same time, pastors are able to live a Life of Worship openly in the Confluence, giving those in their faith community a positive example of what a balanced life directed by the King looks like (life-sized modeling). A balanced life means that sometimes people do not come to functions of the Christian community because they recognize and are tending to God's other gifts and responsibilities—being with a friend who needs to talk, getting much-needed rest, or spending time with family. The more we embrace a life in Christ that reflects this balance, the more we can reverse compartmentalization in the lives of Christians.

While this change is hard and frightens most of us, it is an improvement. In fact, when we reverse the compartmentalization of our lives and begin a Life of Worship, we find new hope for living in the Confluence. The Church will find new opportunities to grow from within and without. By removing the self-made walls between communities in a Christian's life and allowing the Island to pervade all of her communities, we are in essence lessening the importance of "what" she is doing and elevating the importance of the people with whom she is interacting. This seamlessness of life does not diminish the fact that there are things that Christians should avoid; once again, we should be reminded that King Jesus defines how we are to live our lives. We are to be in the world, not of the world. This model allows the Christian to acknowledge the Other in all her communities. She is now able to bridge the great communication gap created by the Confluence.

Earlier I stated that two people are unlikely to view the world in the exact same way unless they are in the exact same part of the Confluence. Nancy's moment in the vegan restaurant served as an example. The Confluence creates real problems with fruitful communication. Most people can float through the Confluence completely unaware that others do not understand their communication, assumptions, and ideas in the way they might think—because the people's participation in the Confluence is driven by their own desires and has little or nothing to do with others, beyond how they fit into individuals' Divine Dreams. Contrast that with a Christian on the Island who is living a Life of Worship. When she is in a community, she first considers the will of the King, then how the King's will affects the others in the community, and *then* her role in that will. For her, then, thorough, fruitful communication becomes incredibly important because her participation in a community no longer is about her own consumption of that community but about having the opportunity to give others a glimpse of God's will and character. In order to practice fruitful communication, she must be involved in the lives and communities of others. We can see this in a night of Nancy's life.

Nancy has never really been a "night-life" person. Todd is, though, so, even though she is a little tired and relatively ambivalent about bluegrass music, she has been looking forward to tonight. The small bar, from the street, does not appear to have enough space for a band to play. She guesses about 120 people are there, probably pushing the limits of the fire code. She imagines how miserable it must have been to breathe there before the smoking ban; she thinks about how sometimes the government does something right.

Todd has been holding her to the deal they made about trying to figure out a way to stop the animal cruelty at Meyers Packing, so they have been spending a lot more time together. She notices over time that he is always listening to bluegrass. Of the little Nancy hears through Todd, she notices how often the lyrics are religious in nature. It makes for some interesting conversations between the two of them.

They talk about it once in a while, so, when they are sharing weekend plans with each other, Nancy isn't surprised that Todd, first of all, knows where a live bluegrass band was playing and, second, is going. She doesn't invite herself along, per se, but she does make it quite clear that she is interested in going with him.

At one point during the show, she notices her foot tapping, her hand patting her thigh, and her head nodding along; she is really enjoying the music. The guy next to her leans over and yells over the music, "These guys are really tight! They sound a lot like the Dillards!"

Nancy has no idea what he is talking about, so she smiles and yells back, "Yeah!" With that, she makes her way to the bar to get a drink. The room grows quiet as the band finishes a song, and she hears someone mumble from the front, "Thanks so much fer com ouw nigh. We are the Moon Pie Hefe. Back in bough ten mins."

Todd comes by a second later and asks her to order him a beer while he gets in line for the restroom. Nancy settles in at the now-bustling bar and waits for the attention of the harried bartender.

"You would think we would be served quickly so that we could start playing again sooner." The guy isn't really speaking to anyone in particular, but, since he is between Nancy and the bar server's entrance, Nancy out of reflex looks over at him. She is startled to realize it is the banjo player from the band.

"You guys sound great tonight!"

"Thanks, we have been working hard for this show. This is the first time we aren't just doing covers but originals, too."

"Well, it shows. But I thought your name was the Moon Shines Heavy? That guy a second ago said it was the Moon Pie Hefe."

"Ha! That was me. I tend to mumble. It is the Moon Shines Heavy." He smiles and extends his hand. "I'm Jake—nice to meet you."

"Nice to meet you too, Jake. I'm Nancy," she replies as she shakes his hand. "You know, you guys sound a lot like the Dillards. Really tight," she says, trying to hold back a smirk.

Jake grins big and becomes very interested. "You think so? In what ways? I have been trying to tell the guys that our original stuff sounds a lot like the Dillards."

"You caught me, Jake. This is my first bluegrass show. My friend is the one who is really into it, and I am here with him. I really do think you guys sound great and am having a wonderful time, but I have no idea who the Dillards are. Some guy yelled that at me about five minutes ago. But Todd, my friend, could probably tell you about how you guys sound like the Dillards. He really loves bluegrass and knows all about it. He's having a great time, too. Right now he is the neverending line to the restroom."

"Oh, that's cool. We all gotta start somewhere, and at least you're here and not at home watching TMZ. You probably could have faked your way through that conversation if you wanted to. Say, I have to go play again soon—are you and your boyfriend going to stick around for the next set? I actually would like to pick his brain for a fresh perspective."

Nancy thinks about correcting Jake and telling him that Todd isn't her boyfriend. She doesn't want to seem like she is trying to hit on him, though, so she lets it slide. She also hasn't been nearly as into celebrity gossip as she used to be, but the TMZ remark still kind of stung. "If I tell him you want his opinion about bluegrass, I don't think there is any way he will let us leave early." She doesn't exactly want to stay out that late, especially with Bible study so early tomorrow, but this would be really important to Todd. "I'll tell you what. I will let Todd know that you want his opinion if you will tell me two things later: why so many bluegrass songs sound religious and what you meant by that TMZ remark."

"Uh, sure!," he responds but looks intently beyond Nancy. "That sounds fair." He starts to turn away from the bar. "Nancy, this beautiful young woman who commands the attention of the room is my girlfriend, Loraine."

A pretty redhead walks up and gives Jake a kiss, saying, "You're playing so well!"

"Nancy: Loraine, my better half. Loraine: Nancy, bluegrass novice. Ladies, I will see you soon." After finally getting a handful of Old Milwaukees for the band, Jake makes his way back to the little stage.

One of the primary things we need for fruitful communication is time to serve God, of which we now have an abundant amount, thanks to a Life of Worship. We need all this time because, after observing the Confluence, we know we no longer can assume anything about anyone else in our communities. Since we cannot assume, we must actually listen and find out what they believe, how they see the world, and how they define terms. Take the example of Jake and Nancy. They met in the Confluence in a shared community. We have followed their stories from the beginning, and we can see that, in order for them to communicate thoroughly, a lot of terms and ideas need to be defined. Their perspectives differ because the other communities they take part in are very different.

We see that Nancy is trying to live her life in a way that gives her opportunities to be with people. In doing so, she can then share with them what she believes and how she sees the world through agreed-on definitions of terms. If we want our communication to be received the way we intend, we have to approach giving others a glimpse of God's will as an ongoing *discussion*, not a lecture.[71] The ongoing discussion of God's will is then paired with life-sized modeling of the ideas, assumptions, and core values (the King's filter) of the Kingdom Community.

You probably realize that these deeper connections do not happen overnight or through one conversation. Communicating effectively not only applies to spreading the Gospel outside of the Church but also must take place with those we assume *already* understand and agree with us. We are doing a great disservice to the people in our Christian communities by assuming that, since they are in a community, they agree with or understand all of that for which it stands. Most do not, and our current ways of communication are not helping the problem.

One thing leaders in the Church can do is use consistent language, from the pulpit, in meetings, and in conversation. No matter how trivial it may seem, take time occasionally to define terms and concepts you use as part of your consistent language—in the pulpit, in meetings, in conversation. When you use a term or concept that is not regularly used, define it. Whenever the opportunity is appropriate, ask others how they define the consistent language you use. This will be a change in behavior for most of us, but it is a big step in the direction of fruitful communication.

Like Nancy, we also need to invest in real relationships with people. To do so, we need to dip into the Confluence with them and invite them to be part of our communities. That leads to a hard truth: sometimes this is going to be enjoyable! Living a Life of Worship brings about a lot of good times. You will look forward to hanging out with people and getting to know them better. The deeper conversations you will have and opportunities to serve people in everyday situations will start to pile up in your life. Of course, not all of them will be great. Sometimes you won't want to see people or go out, but you will still go because people you care about will be there. Every time you see them is another opportunity to give them a glimpse of God's will and for the Holy Spirit to work.

Seeing life this way reflects a model of mission and service that most Christian communities currently do not have because of the impact of the Confluence. While Christian communities establish special mission and service projects—and should do so—most allow their people to see such opportunities as only special, designated times in life. The Life of Worship allows for the everyday happenings of a Christian's life to be opportunities for mission and service. Once again, when the groove of the Island pervades the life of a Christian, the "what" and "when" become far less important than the "who." When that bulb lights up above your head and the idea of a Life of Worship clicks, you probably will think, "Sweet molasses, I am in the mission field every day of my life!" At the same time, you will be able to see evidence of how God already has been working every day in your life to touch others.

In order for the Church to counteract the challenges in the Confluence, it needs to start poking holes in the walls of compartmentalization. We need to become "outies" instead of "innies." We have observed that in the Confluence most people are not inclined to treat the Kingdom Community as an Island but treat another community as an island, usually their favorite type of Christian community. It becomes the community where they "get God," so, as in any other community, participants customize their community activities and commitment levels to their specific tastes. When they have an activity or community that they want God to bless, they bring it into their Christian community. If they have people who they want to "get God," too, they bring them to their Christian community. This is the way of the Confluence, not the way of the Island of the Kingdom Community. In general, Christians fit this model:

Confluence→ Christian community→ Island of the Kingdom Community (ideally) →Stop

We need to change that to:

Island of the Kingdom Community→ Christian Community→ Confluence→ "Rinse and Repeat"

"Rinse and repeat" is a familiar directive from the backs of shampoo bottles, but it works here too. As the Spirit and the Word work through the individual living out the groove in the Confluence, others are swept up onto the Island by the King. Those people now find their identity in their baptism (rinse), then they repeat the cycle.

Poking holes in compartmentalization and living "out" the Island go hand in hand. We turn to Nancy's and Jake's stories one last time.

> Once Todd hears about Nancy's conversation with Jake, he is excited. The two of them stick around after the last set to talk with Jake, Loraine, and few other members of the band. Jake and Todd really hit it off. While they chatter away about the intricacies of bluegrass, Nancy and Loraine have their own conversation as they try to follow along.
>
> Eventually, Todd checks his watch and says they should get going. Nancy is somewhat relieved, as it already was late for her. After he and Jake exchange information to get together and talk bluegrass again, Todd and Nancy get up and say their goodbyes.

As Nancy is shaking Jake's hand, Jake says, "You know, Nancy, I don't hate TMZ. I watch it once in a while myself." Nancy gives a genuine smile as Jake goes on. "We never got to your question about bluegrass and religion. I guess you'll have to come back."

"You got it. I had a lot of fun tonight!" Nancy replies.

After a few more pleasantries, they leave.

On the drive home Todd takes his eyes off the road for second to look at Nancy. "Thank you," he says.

"For what?"

"For everything tonight. For coming to the show. For having a good time and hanging out. For just being you." Nancy feels her cheeks flush a little. He continues, "I'm sorry we are out so late. I know you have Bible study early tomorrow, and that is really important to you."

"Oh, it's okay. I'll just miss it. I'll be more rested for worship that way. If I don't go, it isn't like Jesus is going to disown me or anything. I go because it is good for me and I enjoy it. Besides, I wouldn't be putting what I learn there into practice if I made us leave early."

Todd wants more information. "What do you mean by that?"

Nancy seizes the opportunity. "Well, to follow Jesus is to put other people before me. That's what He does; He put you and me before Himself by dying on the cross so that we could live with him forever in His kingdom. Most of what I learn in Bible study is how He did that or how I can put him and other people first in my life."

"How—I mean, why?" Todd wants to ask more but isn't sure how. "I'm just curious how you think this works."

Nancy gives him a very simple gospel statement and asks him to ask her specific questions about it. It is a good drive home for her. This is the first time Todd has been openly curious.

Three weeks later, the Moon Shines Heavy is playing another show. Todd and Nancy have plans to grab some food with Jake and Loraine beforehand. Nancy decides to try something Pastor Paul has been encouraging the congregation to do. He's been asking people to invite friends from church to things they may not have in common, so she invites Beth, a good friend from Bethlehem, to the show.

Todd had meant Beth once before at a kayaking race, and they got along well. Nancy tells Todd she has invited Beth to the show, and she is wondering whether anyone would mind her joining them for dinner, too. Todd says he doesn't think it's a problem.

Jake and Loraine meet the three of them in the waiting area of Tres Hermanos—one of Jake and Loraine's favorite Mexican restaurants. Pleasantries are exchanged, then they discuss the tewnty-minute wait for a table. Beth says, "It will be worth it; the food here is great!" A conversation ensues about who has or hasn't eaten there and at other favorite restaurants.

When they are seated, Loraine sits next to Beth. Loraine inquires, "So, Beth, how do you know Todd and Nancy?"

Beth replies, "Well, I have only met Todd once"—her voice turns to a whisper as she looks at Nancy and hurriedly says—"but Nancy talks about him all the time, so I feel like I know him pretty well." She begins to speak at a normal level again. "I know Nancy from church."

Loraine is visibly taken aback by the last part, but she asks, "Oh, really, what church?"

"Bethlehem Baptist Church over on Springbrook." Beth says matter-of-factly.

"Oh, I think have driven past there. Baptist, you say? I think my mom was Baptist. I wasn't raised anything—so I could make my own choices."

Beth thinks about defending being Baptist but instead asks, "Where did you grow up?

Loraine starts into her life story as Beth asks questions to get to know her better. The whole group talks and laughs and gets acquainted. After dinner, they go to the venue early so that Jake can get ready. Before, Todd, Nancy, and Beth were just going to a show, but now, along with Loraine, they each feel they are there to support Jake.

The Moon Shines Heavy takes the small stage, and, as they begin to play, Nancy looks at Todd, Loraine, and Beth. She smiles and prays silently, *"Thanks, God. You are good. Bless this night."*

Nancy is poking holes in her walls all over the place. She thinks it is important for Todd to talk to Jake, even though she will miss Bible study because of it. She even sees her doing so as a result of her Bible Study! She brings the Island to Todd in her conversation and her actions. She talks about how her Christian community is important for her and how it helps her understand the groove.

Nancy then intentionally brings her Christian community into the Confluence by inviting Beth along. Beth is then able to help Nancy live out the groove in the Confluence. In the end, Nancy recognizes that going to a bluegrass show can be part of a Life of Worship. She is becoming Free to Serve.

In general, Nancy is beginning to realize that her entire life is an opportunity for service and mission. She sees how she has been given the chance to give people in her life a glimpse of God's will and character. She is breaking down the walls separating the communities in her life in an intentional way. Her secondary communities begin to mix, but the common thread among them all is the Island of the Kingdom Community. She sees her vocation and responsibilities in a new light, as well: they are not things that get in the way of life but opportunities to live out the groove. This slow change in attitude and behavior is encouraged farther when she can look back at her life and see God moving.

Some may realize that living out the Church in this way just will not work with the current structure of many Christian communities. Freedom can be frightening when some streams of Christianity are turning inward out of fear of dwindling numbers and the "anything-goes" bogeyman of this transitional era of thought. Leaders may have an insecure feeling about not doing enough "churchy things" to meet their perceived quota. Success in this model is not measured by the number of ministries or the number of people participating in them. Leaders' schedules will still have tasks, but an increasing amount of time will be devoted to people and how to spend more time with them. (Imagine how this increased outside-the-office interaction could help pastors write sermons that connect with listeners.)

Living a Life of Worship likely will have a huge impact on the life and role of many leaders. If so, it undoubtedly will have a substantial impact on how they structure their communities and run their day-to-day operations. Christian communities are unique, so they will change in different ways. For many, though, the changes could be drastic. Here are just a few examples: leaders likely would have less time in the office. Owing to the reduction of ministries, overhead costs would be lower, and coordinating the calendar and facilities would take less time. Most people in the community would be likely to know each other better and be involved in each other's lives, so people who fit very Modern-Individualistic profiles probably would leave. Pastors would spend a lot more time meeting with people inside and outside the Christian community, even without illnesses or problems necessitating those meetings. Most communities probably would not have enough people filling the pastoral role to accommodate these changes in their Christian communities and would need to explore ways to address that issue.

With structural change or vocational definition within the Church, we need to remember that we have options. The way we do things now is just the way we do things now. Our structures and approaches may have worked wonderfully in a previous era, but that era is passing away. The Church needs to be willing to change the things in its communities that can be customized according to the groove of King Jesus. Regardless of whether some are ready to admit it, the King has left to us a great deal to customize in most Christian communities. The transition to being Free to Serve and to living a Life of Worship may seem difficult, but we should not let the opportunity pass and must be willing to do the hard work.

Conclusion

Considering the Fluid Confluence of Communities enables us to see its strengths and challenges and observe the relatively recent development of our thought processes. We can see how our ideas of identity and individuality affect our everyday decisions. We realize that our pursuit of the Divine Dream affects how we see ourselves and how we see community playing a role in our lives.

Once we observe these things, we can see how the Island of the Kingdom Community should be our dry ground in the Confluence. That realization has tremendous implications for how we live out the life of the Church. We have a simple yet challenging change to make: we must give up *our* Divine Dream and yield to *King Jesus' Divine Plan*. In order to do so, we must reclaim the identity of our baptism into Christ's death and resurrection, become thorough communicators, break down the walls of compartmentalization, and enable the Church to live out the groove of the Island in the Confluence.

King Jesus has given us the freedom to hope. He has given us the filter of how to live in this world, regardless of cultural pressures or external circumstances. To borrow a phrase from Scripture, we cannot continue to put new wine into old wineskins. We are in a transitional era, and the Church has the opportunity to influence the next era. When we work within the Confluence and live out the groove, we show the world how the Kingdom Community is *the* Island for Christians.

We now have an idea of the direction in which we must head. We can emphasize that King Jesus forms our identities on the Island; they are not found within ourselves. We can improve our communication and actually be on the same page with people within our communities. We can change our structure and become "outies" in order to bring the ways of the Island into the Confluence. We must try to break down the walls of compartmentalization and reclaim the Life of Worship. We have hope. If we work together and chase after the will of God, the Spirit will pull us along. It can be done.

The ideas within this book are just the start of a discussion that needs to continue. As you ponder your role in that discussion, I leave you with a few of the words we began with.

> The Bride of Christ, the Church, will not die out or fade. It will continue to flourish, grow, and take shapes we may never have imagined. Jesus is faithful and keeps His promises. We need to follow Him wherever He leads, work with what He has given us, and look as He describes.

Appendix:
How to Engage Others
in the Confluence: Foundational Elements

This guide is only that—a guide, a tool to help those of us who find breaking out of our individualism difficult. It is purposefully devoid of 'Island in the Confluence' terminology so that it is useful to those who have not been exposed to such ideas. It should be evident, however, that it does contain some of the practical applications of the principles found in the book.

This guide is by no means complete, although it should get your mind thinking about opportunities to engage others. I hope it gives you confidence and courage to engage others for the Kingdom and live out your Life of Worship.

Step 1: Getting Started: What is holding you back from engaging people?

Step 2: How to start a conversation and a new relationship.

Step 3: We are talking, so now what?

Step 4: How to engage people you already know, and possibly know very well.

Step 1: Getting Started: What is holding you back from engaging people?

First, **pray**, pray, pray. **Chase after the will of God. Immerse** yourself in the **Scriptures** and become a willing **servant** of **Christ**.

Remember that it is **love** that makes you approach people. Love that understands that you need to put yourself out there. Love that is sacrificial and humble. Love that is about the recipient not the giver. I am not saying that this is easy, but remember to love. Everything else falls into place.

You have nothing to lose. The only things holding you back from talking to people are your fear and pride.

> *What will I say?*
>> This guide will hopefully give you some starting points.
> *I don't want to look stupid.*
>> This is totally understandable. Some people have multiple reasons they don't want to talk to someone else. Most are afraid that other people will stump them with some sort of argument that they know nothing about. You can always say you don't know the answer to a perplexing question.
> *What if the person doesn't want to talk?*
>> Then the person doesn't want to talk. It happens. Simply let the conversation end; don't be pushy.

Do not engage someone in conversation unless you are willing for that person to become part of your life.

This is a hard one—and it may be part of the fear that people have about engaging others, although it probably isn't identified. When you talk to someone else, you are inviting yourself into the person's life. This of course needs to be reciprocal if you are going to be genuine. You want to be genuine. Remember: the goal here is to share the good news of Jesus and plant the seeds of new life for the person you are talking to. If this happens, this person will be your adopted brother or sister. In other words, the very heart of the purpose of engaging someone else is a **lasting relationship.**

The benefit of remembering this point is manifold. Many folks are put off by the idea of engaging others by the sheer enormity of the task. *"I don't have time." "I am not a church worker." "I can't reach that many people."*

> But think of it this way: Say you talk to 15 people over the course of a month. Some are new relationships, and some are existing relationships. Of those 15, three are receptive to your friendship—knowing full well that you are a Christian (more on that later). That gives you three new people in your life—not a horribly hectic number. You can become closer to those folks over time, letting the relationships grow organically, with you being the best, most inclusive friend you can be. Let's say in a year or two one person becomes a follower of Jesus; that person can now do the same thing that you have done, entering into relationships with three people. Now there are six who have been engaged. This process lends itself to multiplication that at first grows slowly, but over time has the potential to explode.

Don't worry; it isn't as hard as you think.

> You've begun conversations before, you just haven't noticed because it wasn't hard. The difficulty comes from the intentionality.

> *I don't want to seem like I have an agenda.*
>> Everyone has an agenda. Agendas are not bad things; rather, hiding them from people is. Be straightforward about who you are and what your purpose is if it comes up in the conversation. Chances are, it will. If you are genuinely interested in them and their friendship, then your "agenda" is more than trying to "convert" them. You are therefore less threatening.

Overall, remember first these three general truths: People tend to like to talk about themselves and the things they are interested in. People usually are more than happy to give you their opinion on pretty much anything. Others won't really care about your opinion until they know that you care about theirs.

Engaging someone who has interests or background similar to yours is always easier. Of course, that doesn't mean you shouldn't try talking to all types of people. Who knows whether you have common interests until you engage a person in conversation?

Step 2: How to start a conversation and new relationship:

This may seem like the most daunting part of engaging someone because it takes getting over fear and pride. Different situations call for different tactics.

> If you are someplace new, you can ask if the person is familiar with the place.

> If you are familiar with a place and you notice a person is often there as well, you may already have a shared community. This conversation could start off with, "I noticed that you are here almost as much as I am—what brings you here?

> You can always ask someone how things are going, although this question can easily turn into an exchange of pleasantries that ends quickly.

> The basic premise is to start with a question that doesn't facilitate a one-word answer. Try to pick up something in the person's answer and ask the person a question about it. If you have something to add, make it brief. The goal is to get the person talking. Now, you **don't** want to **interrogate the person,** so don't be too pushy. Try to discern the person's comfort level. You don't have to become friends with everyone the first time you talk to them. In fact, that really isn't feasible. You simply want to come off as someone who is interested in him and who is a good listener. If it is possible, especially if you are not sure

you will see the person again, try at the end of the conversation to arrange to talk with him again.

Step 3: We are talking, so now what?

Once engaged in conversation, ask the person her opinion on God, religion, or a hot-button topic of the day. This should get her talking but may also make her suspicious of you. If she asks why you ask, be straightforward. Time to unleash the agenda: *You think it is important that people talk about these things.* That may be all you need to say at the start. The hope is that she will ask you what you think or believe. Make it simple: *You believe Jesus is God, and that means a whole bunch of things about how you see the world.*

Such a statement undoubtedly will lead to debate on issues like religious tolerance, gay marriage, abortion, gun rights, the "church," and so forth. This is a fantastic place to be in the conversation because now you show that you really care about who she is. You also have the chance to share some of your views. Here is where you flip a normally frustrating situation because of differing views. Tell the person that you care what she thinks, but, to really understand her, you need to know her presuppositions or worldview. In other words, what is the *foundation* for the way she thinks? Make sure you take time to define the terms both of you are using.

What is great about this is that **many people have never really thought it through**. You get to help people discover why they think the way they think. This is the part of the conversation that you can have somewhat prepared: you should have a pretty good idea of your presuppositions or worldview, which should focus on Jesus and what He means to the world. Forgiveness of sins can be the focus, but even that isn't at the heart of Christianity. **Christianity centers on the fact that God is**

actually God, and He is involved in the world—and that Jesus is God. Everything flows from that.

If you have trouble putting words to this, that is fine. Just think about it a little: your worldview statement should not be long or complicated. As your lens for the world around you, it is what complicates things. Helping someone recognize or understand her lens can be a lengthy conversation in itself. Not only can you share the Gospel, but also you can **set an understanding between you and the person**—that, unless people's worldview and presuppositions are exactly the same, they will not agree on everything. Debate and converse about big, important things, and try to understand each other better. Realize, though, that it is all right to disagree in the end. It's not a conversation you need to "win." The beauty of this approach is that you are then able unashamedly to pepper the conversations with Gospel and the narrative of the hope of the world. Now, remember love. This understanding does not give you the right to browbeat the person with the Gospel or Law or not to listen. Instead, love her. Love her and let the Gospel be found in your words and actions. Share the Spirit with her. Let the Spirit change her mind.

Step 4: How to engage people you already know—and possibly know very well.

Engaging people you already know is probably more difficult to do than expressing what you believe to strangers.

Part of the reason this is difficult is that you may have already established a pattern of behavior that does not include talking about Jesus, God, or anything spiritual.

The first thing to do is identify whether the person you wish to engage is a person of faith.

If so, does he profess to be a Christian? If the person is Christian, then the opening is rather easy: *"How's it been going where you worship?"* The person could just answer with "fine," so then ask something like *"How did you end up at that church?" "How is your walk?"*

At some point the person will ask you about your "sudden" interest in religion or spirituality. Be honest: your faith has become increasingly important to you, and you believe that God is bigger, more important, and more involved than you used to think. You care about this person—be so bold as to say that you love him—and you believe you know some of the answers as to why we are here and who God is. You feel that this person needs to know this, too. One thing I have found to work well is letting the person know that you were praying and that he kept coming to mind—so you thought you should check in with him. That statement should be true, though. I am confident that, if you know this person and have a habit of prayer, the statement is true.

> If the person is **"religious" but not Christian**, you could begin with *"How did you become _____?"* This opens the door to more conversation. You could then lead into the conversation about presuppositions and worldviews. Take care not to diminish their beliefs. There is a difference between being direct that you believe Jesus is the true and only Son of God (a statement that separates Christianity from all other religions) and trivializing someone else's beliefs who hasn't been blessed with faith in Jesus yet.

> If the **person** professes **no faith,** the conversation may seem quite awkward at first. Several approaches are possible, but one of my favorites is **mentioning that the person came up during your prayer time.** Think about it: that statement tells him first that you are a person of faith and, second, that you and God care about him.

You may be thinking, "Okay, I told the person that I thought about him during a prayer—now what?

Ask the person if everything is all right. Chances are that he will say "yes." (People tend to avoid being vulnerable). Here, *you* have an opportunity to be vulnerable. You can explain how you lean on—better yet, are carried by—God and what that means. Move to your worldview and presuppositions. Ask the person what his worldview and presuppositions are.

You may be avoiding this conversation because you think it will **change** things in **your relationship**. The hope is that **it will**—that actually is what you want. Put your cards face-up on the table. If this affects the way you behave around him, then good; that means that you both are now cognizant that you are a follower of Jesus and are supposed to reflect God to the world around you. Things *will* change. Put it into God's hands, and He won't mess it up!

Last, **pray**, pray, pray. **Chase after the will of God. Immerse** yourself in the **Scriptures,** and become a willing **servant** of **Christ**.

About the Author

After receiving a Master of Divinity from Concordia Seminary in St. Louis, Marc Engelhardt was ordained in 2009 in the Lutheran Church-Missouri Synod. He is passionate about the Church and applying the theology and history of the past two thousand years to today's context. He currently serves as pastor of Reconcile Church, a church-plant in Milwaukee, Wisconsin, where he lives with his wife, Lauren, and dog, Scooter.

Bibliography

Crowell, Steven. "Existentialism." Winter 2010. *The Stanford Encyclopedia of Philosophy.* Ed. Edward N. Zalta. 2012. <http://plato.stanford.edu/archives/win2010/entries/existentialism/>.

Hiebert, Paul G. *Transforming Worldviews, An Anthropological Understanding Of How People Change.* Baker Publishing Group, 2008.

Hume, David. *A Treatise of Human Nature.* Ed. L. A. Selby-Bigge and P. H. Nidditch. 2nd. Oxford: Clrendon Press, 1975.

Hume, David. *Enquiry Concerning the Principles of Morals, Oxford: Clarendon Press, 1975. P. 175.* Ed. L. A. Selby-Bigge and P. H. Nidditch. 3rd. Oxford: Clarendon Press, 1975.

Hume, David. "The Natural History of Religion." Ed. H. E. Root. Stanford: Stanford University Press, 1967.

Locke, John. "The Second Treatise of Civil Government." 2011. *Constitution Society.* February 2012. <http://www.constitution.org/jl/2ndtr02.htm>.

McDonald, William. "Søren Kierkegaard." Summer 2009. *The Stanford Encyclopedia of Philosophy.* Ed. Edward N. Zalta. 2012. <http://plato.stanford.edu/archives/sum2009/entries/kierkegaard/>.

Merriam Webster Online. http://www.merriam-webster.com/dictionary/ individualism. 2012. 13 February 2012.

Morris, William Edward. "David Hume." Fall 2011. *The Stanford Encyclopedia of Philosophy.* Ed. Edward N. Zalta. 2012. < http://plato. stanford.edu/archives/fall2011/entries/hume/>.

Nietzsche, Friedrich. "On the Genealogy of Morals." 1997-2012. *Great Literature Online.* 2012. <http://nietzsche.classicauthors.net/ GenealogyMorals/GenealogyMorals67.html>.

Uzgalis, William. "John Locke." Vers. (Winter 2010 Edition). 2012. *The Stanford Encyclopedia of Philosophy.* Ed. Edward N. Zalta. <http:// plato.stanford.edu/archives/win2010/entries/locke/>.

Wright, Nicholas Thomas. *The Challenge Of Jesus, Rediscovering Who Jesus Was And Is.* Downer's Groove: InterVarsity Press, 199.

Endnotes

Part One

[1] In order to be purely an observer, one must be absolutely objective. This impossibility is illustrated later in Part One. An interesting thing to note, though, is that the initial goal of the Enlightenment—that is, to be completely objective observers—has actually produced the opposite effect and created incredibly biased judges of knowledge.

[2] If you have ever heard the term "hipster," you likely have an opinion about hipsters. At this point, please remember that we are taking the role of observers, not judges. Much can be said about the term "hipster" and the values and ideals that go along with it, including the apparently obvious hypocrisies that present themselves to the outsider. Here is not the place for such a discussion, and, if the example were not germane, I would not have brought the term, along with its baggage, into the conversation.

[3] Compare and contrast this with the view of the individual in India, which slowly is becoming more modern and has its own issues to deal with. In general, the individual in India is directly connected to the greater community. One's identity is given from outside authority, not individually chosen, and the actions and decisions of the individual are seen as reflections of the family and greater community.

[4] For an interesting take on this, see *Transforming Worldviews*. The interpretation of what the limit of the law is for the individual is anything for which the individual does not get punished. Hiebert, Paul G. *Transforming Worldviews, An Anthropological Understanding Of How People Change*. Baker Publishing Group, 2008.

[5] The primary focus of the historical review is philosophy and, within that, the nature of knowledge and truth (epistemology).

6 "Individualism." Merriam Webster Online Dictionary. 2012. Merriam Webster Online. 13 February 2012 <> http://www.merriam-webster.com/dictionary/individualism

7 Uzgalis, William, "John Locke," *The Stanford Encyclopedia of Philosophy (Winter 2010 Edition)*, Edward N. Zalta (ed.), URL = <http://plato.stanford.edu/archives/win2010/entries/locke/>.

8 ibid

9 ibid

10 ibid

11 ibid

12 Locke, John. "The Second Treatise of Civil Government." *Chap. ii. of the state of nature.6.* Constitution Society, 2011. Web. 13 Feb 2012. <http://www.constitution.org/jl/2ndtr02.htm>.

13 Ibid

14 Uzgalis, William, "John Locke," *The Stanford Encyclopedia of Philosophy (Winter 2010 Edition)*, Edward N. Zalta (ed.), URL = <http://plato.stanford.edu/archives/win2010/entries/locke/>.

15 Hume, David. *A Treatise of Human Nature, edited by L. A. Selby-Bigge, 2nd ed. revised by P.H. Nidditch, Oxford: Clarendon Press, 1975. p. 7*

16 "Metaphysics." Merriam Webster Online Dictionary. 2012. Merriam Webster Online. 13 February 2012 <> http://www.merriam-webster.com/dictionary/metaphysics

17 Morris, William Edward, "David Hume," *The Stanford Encyclopedia of Philosophy (Fall 2011 Edition)*, Edward N. Zalta (ed.), URL = <http://plato.stanford.edu/archives/fall2011/entries/hume/>.

18 Hume, David. "The Natural History of Religion", edited by H. E. Root, Stanford: Stanford University Press, 1967. This work is written in a very sarcastic manner. Hume had a reputation for being an atheist and being antireligious even before he published *Natural History* (Morris, William Edward, "David Hume," *The Stanford Encyclopedia of Philosophy (Fall 2011 Edition)*, Edward N. Zalta (ed.), URL = http://plato.stanford.edu/archives/fall2011/entries/hume/)

19 Hume, David. *Enquiry Concerning the Principles of Morals*, edited by L. A. Selby-Bigge, 3rd edition revised by P. H. Nidditch, Oxford: Clarendon Press, 1975. P. 175

[20] McDonald, William, "Søren Kierkegaard," *The Stanford Encyclopedia of Philosophy (Summer 2009 Edition)*, Edward N. Zalta (ed.), URL = <http://plato.stanford.edu/archives/sum2009/entries/kierkegaard/>.

[21] ibid

[22] ibid

[23] ibid

[24] Crowell, Steven, "Existentialism," *The Stanford Encyclopedia of Philosophy (Winter 2010 Edition)*, Edward N. Zalta (ed.), URL = <http://plato.stanford.edu/archives/win2010/entries/existentialism/>.

[25] Nietzsche, Friedrich. "On the Genealogy of Morals." Great Literature Online. 1997-2012 <http://nietzsche.classicauthors.net/GenealogyMorals/GenealogyMorals67.html>(13 Feb, 2012).

[26] Crowell, Steven, "Existentialism," *The Stanford Encyclopedia of Philosophy (Winter 2010 Edition)*, Edward N. Zalta (ed.), URL = <http://plato.stanford.edu/archives/win2010/entries/existentialism/>.

[27] Nietzsche, Friedrich. "On the Genealogy of Morals." Great Literature Online. 1997-2012 <http://nietzsche.classicauthors.net/GenealogyMorals/GenealogyMorals55.html> (13 Feb, 2012).

[28] As already noted, the line cited from the U.S. Constitution is clearly borrowed from Locke's life, liberty, health and possessions.

[29] In addition to popular media, the educational system is raising awareness: revised history books recognize the wrongs done in the name of progress. It is also being reflected in popular media.

[30] This is evident in Western movies: from the beginning of the cinematic era until the 1970s, one of the most common motifs in film was cowboys versus Indians, wherein cowboys and pioneers are heroes and Native Americans are villains.

[31] "Discovered" is a shorthand term for "observed and experienced."

[32] From here on, the phrase "life, liberty, and the pursuit of happiness" will be replaced by the term "Divine Dream." I was careful not to use "American Dream," as the term is too narrow and confining: these desires are not bound geographically to the United States. The Dream is divine both because it is considered a God-given right and because the individual becomes the god of his own reality.

[33] The statement is certainly hyperbolized and does not apply to all; however, individualism exists in degrees, and some people will do whatever they see fit, within societal standards (legally) or outside of what is acceptable in society (illegally), in order to experience the full extent of their "rights."

[34] If an individual intends to communicate his needs or desires, he first must recognize the Other beyond himself, then he must come to a consensus with the Other as to what gestures, symbols, or noises mean (standards of communication). Otherwise, his needs or desires will remain unfulfilled. The Other shapes and influences how he communicates and in turn shapes and influences him.

[35] This idea is covered thoroughly in Part Three, "The Fluid Confluence of Communities."

Part Two

[1] I have tested this theory since then, and, for the most part, it seems to hold true. The issue is not whether one uses Facebook, but whether one sees it as useful and why.

[2] By most accounts we are, at most, 45 years into this era—not a very long time. To put it into perspective, that is about two generations. It normally takes three generations for immigrants to lose a close connection to their native country, so it stands to reason that it would take at least three generations for a way of thought to take hold or die out. Compound that with the fact that a very small percentage of the population started thinking differently 45 years ago, and it makes sense that we are actually transitioning and not completely in a different era. With the ease of worldwide communication, however, I have to imagine that this transition era will be brief in the scope of world history.

[3] Many people also do not think Modernism is a problem and in fact are resistant to the changing era.

[4] Genesis 2, 3:8

Part Three

[1] I actually know this to be true after having conversations with people whom I now call friends.

[2] The Free to Serve section contains more on the topic of communication in the Fluid Confluence of Communities.

[3] People often participate in communities with the goal of changing and becoming something different. Weight Watchers, Alcoholics Anonymous,

and the military are examples of such communities. Individuals seek them out because they offer the individual's desired outcome; the individual is willing to submit to the requirements of the chosen community. Even so, when such communities require more of the person than the individual is willing to commit, or the community does not fulfill the initial desire of the person, then the individual will become suspicious and distance herself from the community. These types of communities can easily become islands for an individual, becoming the filter for interaction with the rest of the Confluence. When this occurs, her identity becomes wrapped up in that specific community. While it is an island for her, she may still be suspicious of that community's control over her, but to a far lesser degree.

4   As stated in the Summary Analysis of Part One, this perception of individual identity is largely misguided, as the communities of which we are or have been a part are constantly shaping and influencing us.

5   The annexation of faith to the private sphere is another product of the Enlightenment.

Part Four

1   The narrative of Genesis is an important foundation for the rest of Scripture.

2   Exodus, Leviticus, Numbers, and Deuteronomy contain these instructions.

3   Dr. Joel Biermann, systematics professor at Concordia Seminary, St. Louis, describes the "groove" as the way God designed creation to work. Following the Law does not lead to salvation; rather, it allows one to fit into the "groove" of life the way God meant it to be. I respectfully borrow the term for the purposes of this book.

4   Deuteronomy 28:1–6

5   Isaiah 9:6–7

6   Isaiah 32:1–5

7   "Christ" in Greek

8   Mark 1:14-15

9   N.T.Wright concludes his argument that the call to repent and believe was not just to turn from specific sins, but a call to the people once again to be God's people and let Him be the leader of the Kingdom, rather than try to enter or build the Kingdom by their own devices. Wright, Nicholas Thomas. *The Challenge Of Jesus, Rediscovering Who Jesus Was And Is*. Downer's Grove, IL: InterVarsity Pr, 1999. 52-53.

10 See also Mark 14:61-65 for a clear connection.

11 Mark 10:32–34

12 Galatians 2:20

13 Certain scholars wrestle with this issue: some stress that the Church should not necessarily be afraid of differing interpretations, as long as those interpretations are done within the community of the Christian Church and take into account the rich historical interpretations. At the same time, not every interpretation should be accepted or even entertained.

14 Shema is the first Hebrew word in Deuteronomy 6:4-5. It is an imperative verb that means *hear*.

15 Deuteronomy 6:4-5

16 1 Peter 2:9-10

17 This brings up the concept of "now and not yet," the paradox in which Christians live. We are now saved and freed from sin because of Christ; however, the fullness of what that means has not yet been realized, as we still sin and live in a sinful world.

18 The Kingdom Community and the rest of the Fluid Confluence are all within the Kingdom of God.

19 Lutheran theology does not stop at righteousness, but the popular application of Lutheran theology today often does.

Part Five

1 "Catholic" here has the meaning "universal Christian Church."

2 The streams of Christianity are not only denominations but also nondenominational communities, in that they encompass all manifestations of Christian community that are subject to King Jesus and His Kingdom.

3 I understand the arguments on both sides in the filioque controversy. Its inclusion or exclusion need not negate the confessional unity this creed can give the Kingdom Community.

4 "Catholic" here has the meaning "universal Christian Church."

5 Using a creed presents two challenges. First, some streams of Christianity do not use creeds. This may occur for several reasons but the most prominent are lack of belief in what the creeds say and outright refusal to show unity with the rest of the Church. Without trying to sound too harsh, I would say that not embracing the traditional understanding of the Nicene Creed creates doubt about exactly what Jesus a person or a church actually embraces. Those who

refuse creeds out of rebellion against the historical Church reject the Island, as well, and likely have turned their stream of Christianity into an idol. The second difficulty arises when people profess the creed without belief in it what it says. This is unavoidable and illustrates the difference between the visible and invisible Church: we can never know what actually is in a person's heart, yet at the same time we need tools to identify our common faith as best we can.

6 Non-Christians' lives, too!

7 Timothy 3

8 Not everyone is sure how to have an actual discussion with others. See the Appendix for a simple guide on how to engage people in the Confluence.

CPSIA information can be obtained at www.ICGtesting.com
Printed in the USA
LVOW041714040812

292917LV00002B/3/P